A to Z for Every Manager in FE

A to Z for Every Manager in FE

Susan Wallace and
Jonathan Gravells

continuum

Continuum International Publishing Group

The Tower Building   80 Maiden Lane
11 York Road   Suite 704
London SE1 7NX   NY 10038

© Susan Wallace and Jonathan Gravells

British Library Cataloguing-in-Publication Data
A catalogue record for this book is available from the British Library.

ISBN: 0 8264 9170 7 (paperback)

Library of Congress Cataloging-in-Publication Data
Wallace, Susan.
A–Z for every manager in FE / Susan Wallace and Jonathan Gravells.
   p. cm.
Includes bibliographical references.
ISBN-13: 978–0–8264–9170–1 (pbk.)
ISBN-10: 0–8264–9170–7 (pbk.)
1. Adult education—Administration. 2. Post secondary education—
Administration. I. Gravells, Jonathan. II. Title. III. Title: A to Z for every
manager in FE. IV. Title: A–Z for every manager in further education.
LC5225.A34W34 2007
374′.12—dc22   2006022349

Typeset by RefineCatch Limited, Bungay, Suffolk
Printed and bound in Great Britain by
Ashford Colour Press Ltd, Gosport, Hampshire

Contents

Series Foreword

THE ESSENTIAL FE TOOLKIT SERIES

Jill Jameson
Series Editor

In the autumn of 1974, a young woman newly arrived from Africa landed in Devon to embark on a new life in England. Having travelled half way round the world, she still longed for sunny Zimbabwe. Not sure what career to follow, she took a part-time job teaching EFL to Finnish students. Enjoying this, she studied thereafter for a PGCE at the University of Nottingham in Ted Wragg's Education Department. After teaching in secondary schools, she returned to university in Cambridge and, having graduated, took a job in ILEA in 1984 in adult education. She loved it: there was something about adult education that woke her up, made her feel fully alive, newly aware of all the lifelong learning journeys being followed by so many students and staff around her. The adult community centre she worked in was a joyful place for diverse multi-ethnic communities. Everyone was cared for, including 90-year-olds in wheelchairs, toddlers in the crèche, ESOL refugees, city accountants in business suits and university-level graphic design students. In her eyes, the centre was an educational ideal, a remarkable place in which, gradually, everyone was helped to learn to be who they wanted to be. This was the Chequer Centre, Finsbury, EC1, the 'red house', as her daughter saw it, toddling in from the crèche. And so began the story of a long interest in further education that was to last for many years . . . why, if they did such good work for so many, were FE centres so under-funded and unrecognized, so under-appreciated?

It is with delight that, 32 years after the above story began, I write the Foreword to *The Essential FE Toolkit*, Continuum's new book series of 24 books on further education (FE) for teachers and college leaders. The idea behind the *Toolkit* is to provide a comprehensive guide to FE in a series of compact, readable books. The suite of 24 individual books is gathered together to provide the practitioner with an overall FE toolkit in specialist, fact-filled volumes designed to be easily accessible, written by experts with significant knowledge and experience in their individual fields. All of the authors have in-depth understanding of further education. But – 'Why is further education important? Why does it merit a whole series to be written about it?' you may ask.

At the Association of Colleges Annual Conference in 2005, in a humorous speech to college principals, John Brennan said that, whereas in 1995 further education was a 'political backwater', by 2005 FE had become 'mainstream'. John recalled that, since 1995, there had been '36 separate Government or Government-sponsored reports or white papers specifically devoted to the post-16 sector'. In our recent regional research report (2006) for the Learning and Skills Development Agency, my co-author Yvonne Hillier and I noted that it was no longer 'raining policy' in FE, as we had described earlier (Hillier and Jameson 2003): there is now a torrent of new initiatives. We thought, in 2003, that an umbrella would suffice to protect you. We'd now recommend buying a boat to navigate these choppy waters, as it looks as if John Brennan's 'mainstream' FE, combined with a tidal wave of government policies will soon lead to a flood of new interest in the sector, rather than end anytime soon.

There are good reasons for all this government attention on further education. In 2004/05, student numbers in LSC-funded further education increased to £4.2m, total college income was around £6.1 billion and the average college had an annual turnover of £15m. Further education has rapidly increased in national significance regarding the need for ever greater achievements in UK education and skills training for millions of learners, providing qualifications and workforce training to feed a UK national economy hungrily in competition with other OECD nations. The 120 recommendations of the Foster Review (2005) therefore in the main encourage colleges to focus their work on vocational skills, social inclusion and achieving academic progress. This series is here to consider all three of these areas and more.

The series is written for teaching practitioners, leaders and managers in the 572 FE/LSC-funded institutions in the UK, including FE colleges, adult education and sixth-form institutions, prison education departments, training and workforce development units, local education authorities and community agencies. The series is also written for PGCE/Cert Ed/City & Guilds Initial and continuing professional development (CPD) teacher trainees in universities in the UK, USA, Canada, Australia, New Zealand and beyond. It will also be of interest to staff in the 600 Jobcentre Plus providers in the UK and to many private training organizations. All may find this series of use and interest in learning about FE educational practice in the 24 different areas of these specialist books from experts in the field.

Our use of this somewhat fuzzy term 'practitioners' includes staff in the FE/LSC-funded sector who engage in professional practice in governance, leadership, management, teaching, training, financial and administration services, student support services, ICT and MIS technical support, librarianship, learning resources, marketing, research and development, nursery and crèche services, community and business support, transport and estates management. It is also intended to include staff in a host of other FE services including work-related training, catering, outreach and specialist health, diagnostic additional learning support, pastoral and religious support for students. Updating staff in professional practice is critically important at a time of such continuing radical policy-driven change, and we are pleased to contribute to this nationally and internationally.

We are also privileged to have an exceptional range of authors writing for the series. Many of our series authors are renowned for their work in further education, having worked in the sector for thirty years or more. Some have received OBE or CBE honours, professorships, fellowships and awards for contributions they have made to further education. All have demonstrated a commitment to FE that makes their books come alive with a kind of wise guidance for the reader. Sometimes this is tinged with world-weariness, sometimes with sympathy, humour or excitement. Sometimes the books are just plain clever or a fascinating read, to guide practitioners of the future who will read these works. Together, the books make up a considerable portfolio of assets for you to take with you through your journeys in further education. We hope the experience of reading the books will be interesting, instructive and pleasurable and that experience gained from them will last, renewed, for many seasons.

It has been wonderful to work with all of the authors and with Continuum's UK Education Publisher, Alexandra Webster, on this series. The exhilarating opportunity of developing such a comprehensive toolkit of books probably comes once in a lifetime, if at all. I am privileged to have had this rare opportunity, and I thank the publishers, authors and other contributors to the series for making these books come to life with their fantastic contributions to FE.

Dr Jill Jameson
Series Editor
March, 2006

Series Introduction

THE ESSENTIAL FE TOOLKIT SERIES
Jill Jameson
Series Editor

A to Z for Every Manager in FE – Susan Wallace and Jonathan Gravells

Welcome to the *A to Z for Every Manager in FE*! If you are worried about the many management demands facing you at a time when more attention than ever is being placed on the further education (FE) system since the Foster Review (2005) and the publication of the government White Paper on FE, *Further Education: Raising Skills, Improving Life Chances* (2006), then this book will help you. From 'A for Accountability' to 'Z for Zero Tolerance', this book has been developed and written specifically for new, aspirant and existing managers in FE at every level nationally, whether staff are in adult education, general FE colleges, sixth-form education, training and/or work-based learning, prison education, youth provision, careers, voluntary and/or community learning. The authors, Sue Wallace and Jonathan Gravells, have extensive experience in and knowledge of the post-compulsory education sector and the multiple challenges facing institutional managers in different contexts. They bring a knowledgeable, skilled, sympathetically humorous approach to the question of management and leadership in FE, guiding us helpfully and wisely through key situations affecting managers.

Sue and Jonathan select the fictional environment of Bogginbrook College as the setting in which to place a series of example issues, scenarios and characters to demonstrate salient points relating to management and leadership practice and theory in FE. The characters in the A to Z are both instructive and amusing: from the disastrous Head of School, Norman, to the supportive but somewhat scary Sarah, Head of Faculty, we have met these people before in the working corridors of our own lives in colleges.

Here, we see them again in ways that help us to understand and cope with the many challenges confronting leaders and managers in FE institutions. If you want a quick dip into an A to Z for managers in FE to update yourself on policy, recent issues and management theory, this book provides a helpful guide.

The authors discuss key dilemmas and difficulties affecting busy managers, grouped under a variety of relevant themes for ease of access, in a well-organized and simple structure. These themes include: *Improving performance, Recruiting and selecting people, Being more effective, Making the most of change,* Demonstrating leadership, *Having productive conversations, Staff development and support, Redicing negative stress, The FE context* and *Gurus and heroes.* The A to Z sections are listed under these themes but also cross-referenced to each other, so there are different ways to read this book: straight through, dipping in and out, or following a particular thread that interests you. Possibly amongst the most challenging issue facing managers in FE is the problem of coping with a very busy workload day-to-day yet also keeping up to date, alive to and optimistic about the many rapid developments happening in FE nationally. This book will help update your thinking on developments in FE at a time when the Foster Review (2005), government White Paper (2006) and Quality Improvement Agency (QIA) are all calling for widespread, rapid improvements in leadership and management across the FE system. The *A to Z for Every Manager in FE* is a book to help and inspire you make the most of these opportunities in informative, entertaining ways. I thoroughly commend it to you.

Dr Jill Jameson
Director of Research
School of Education and Training
University of Greenwich
j.jameson@gre.ac.uk

Introduction

Welcome to this A to Z!

Whether you've just been newly appointed to an FE management role or are an experienced manager wanting a quick update, this book is for you. You'll find that you can use it in a number of ways. You may like simply to dip into it to discover a definition, or to mug up on a particular topic prior to a meeting. Or you may like to do some more concentrated reading with a specific focus by following linked entries to explore one of the themes, such as *Improving performance* or *Making the most of change*, which we map out for you following this Introduction. Perhaps you'll use it to refresh your memory about management theory, or even to remind yourself about the funny side of working as a manager in FE.

In your reading of this *A–Z* you'll encounter certain characters who appear and reappear in the various examples and scenarios. As FE managers they all have their strengths and foibles, and we hope that the process of spotting these will add to your enjoyment of the book. They are there to instruct (by good example or otherwise), but also to entertain. Their triumphs, quandaries and disasters all take place at Bogginbrook College – an entirely fictional institution. We provide an organizational chart at the back of the book so that you can see at a glance how these characters relate to one another in their management roles.

There are some real-life characters in here too. Some are writers and thinkers whose work will be useful to you if you're working as a manager in FE. They include management theorists from the wider world of big business whose ideas have a particular relevance to the corporate bodies which are today's FE colleges. There are key names in FE too; heroes and heroines of the sector. And some are iconic figures who demonstrate that effective performance is still possible even in the most difficult crisis situations – crises even more challenging than some we find ourselves facing in FE. You'll find these – the gurus and the heroes – listed under each letter as appropriate.

For whatever purpose you use this *A–Z* – and we hope you find it helpful in all the ways we've mentioned – do bear in mind that it's intended primarily as a toolkit for busy managers. It makes no claim to be an in-depth textbook. The individual entries are designed to provide rule-of-thumb advice on practical management skills, or working summaries of relevant management theory. The map of linked entries allows you to take your exploration one step further; as do the cross references, indicated in **bold**. But if you'd like to pursue any of these topics or ideas in more depth, you'll find suggestions for further reading incorporated in the text, as well as summarized in the References section at the end of the book.

Themes

Improving performance
A is for Accountability
A is for Appraisal
B is for Benchmarking
B is for Bullying
D is for Disciplinary
F is for Feedback
I is for Interviews
M is for Mentoring and Coaching
P is for Performance Management

Recruiting and selecting people
E is for Equal Opportunities
I is for Interviews
R is for Recruitment
S is for Selection
S is for Succession Crisis

Being more effective
A is for Accountability
D is for Delegation
G is for Getting Organized

J is for JFDI
M is for Managing Upwards
M is for Meetings
O is for Objectives
P is for Paperwork
S is for Stress

Making the most of change

C is for Change
F is for Foster Report
J is for JFDI
K is for Kanter
M is for Mergers
S is for Stress
T is for Transformational Leadership
U is for Updating

Demonstrating leadership

A is for Accountability
A is for Authenticity
B is for Bullying
C is for Consult or Control
E is for Emotional Intelligence
L is for Leadership
O is for Objectives
T is for Transformational Leadership
W is for Walking Around
X is for X-Men
Z is for Zero Tolerance

Having productive conversations

A is for Authenticity
A is for Appraisal
E is for Emotional Intelligence
I is for Interviews
M is for Mentoring and Coaching
N is for Negotiation
P is for Politics

Staff development and support
A is for Appraisal
C is for Consult or Control
F is for Feedback
M is for Mentoring and Coaching
E is for Equal Opportunities
D is for Delegation
O is for Objectives
P is for Performance Management
S is for Succession Crisis

Reducing negative stress
B is for Bullying
G is for Getting Organized
M is for Managing Upwards
M is for Mentoring and Coaching
P is for Paperwork
P is for Politics
S is for Stress
Y is for You
Z is for Zero Tolerance

The FE context
C is for the Cinderella Sector
F is for the Foster Report
F is for Funding
H is for Heroines and Heroes of FE
I is for Inspection
M is for Market
M is for Mergers
S is for Succession Crisis
V is for Vice Principal
W is for White Papers and other milestones

Gurus and heroes
A is for John Adair
B is for Warren Bennis
D is for Peter Drucker
H is for Charles Handy

H is for Heroines and Heroes of FE
K is for Kanter
P is for Colin Powell
S is for Shackleton

A is for Accountability

Given the changes in the FE sector brought about by incorporation and its aftermath, it is perhaps appropriate that our sprint through management concepts and techniques should start here. Theoretically, at least, the process of colleges coming out of local authority control over a decade ago, and becoming free-standing corporations, might be expected to have created greater accountability in individual institutions, with government openly encouraging principals to behave more like the chief executive of a business.

So is it enough simply to tell someone that they are responsible for something? Well, probably not. Like greatness, accountability can be thrust upon you, but it generally works better if you accept, or even seek it.

The dictionary defines accountability as 'being answerable', or 'bound to give an explanation'. It is about taking responsibility, as an individual or a team, for putting things right when they have gone wrong, but it is also about being able to take the credit when things go well. A *lack* of accountability might be characterized by some or all of the following:

A***-covering	'Didn't you read the email?'
Invoking the mythical 'They'	'If only they would tell us what the plan is'
Buck-passing	'If IT had fixed my PC in time, I could have sent you those figures'
Jobsworthing	'It's not my job to tell them the timetable has changed'
Playing victim	'They want me to improve standards, but they never give me the resources to do it'
Coasting	'Don't worry, I'm sure somebody will already have reported that it's not working'

Such attitudes are easy to fall into, because we all have to work with constraints, which we may see as limiting our effectiveness. However much incorporation has increased a college's freedom to act, it is still dependent upon public funding which can leave it under-resourced, and it is subjected to a degree of bureaucracy from outside which may feel intrusive. So how do managers in FE set about creating the conditions for greater accountability in their teams, and maybe adjusting to greater accountability in their own role?

Ensure accountability is accompanied by authority
A recent report by the Learning and Skills Research Centre (*Leadership, development and diversity in the learning and skills sector*, LSRC 2005) found that many college staff felt they had distributed *responsibility*, but not *power*. Senior management teams (SMT) regarded their style as distributed and collegiate, but those who worked for SMT often saw them as operational and transactional in their approach (see **T is for Transformational Leadership**).

Align your team behind an agreed vision and objectives
If you want people to take responsibility for decisions, and to take the initiative in improving performance, it makes sense that they must feel part of a united team. If they have had some involvement in formulating the team's vision and objectives, then the sense of ownership will be even greater. People will be more inclined to accept responsibility in pursuit of common goals, and a future which excites them.

Use measurement and standards to enable people, *not* to control them
It is difficult to be accountable for our performance if we have no means of measuring this. So giving people the tools to measure themselves and get reliable, meaningful feedback is essential. But people who are subjected to constant close monitoring and review from on high learn *not* to take ownership of improving their own performance. Why reflect on what you are doing and find ways to do it even better if someone is already doing this for you? The best measures and standards cover not only quantitative results but also group values and norms of behaviour. With tools like these and clearly agreed objectives, people can take responsibility for

managing themselves (see **D is for Drucker**). They are also more likely to hold each other accountable for sticking to these standards and norms.

Clarify roles and responsibilities

Not surprisingly perhaps, organizational structure can have an impact on whether people feel a clear sense of accountability. We should avoid creating roles which have no real authority or which duplicate and interfere with each other. But it is equally important to ensure that everyone in the structure understands where their own responsibilities lie, and what responsibilities may be shared. Getting this wrong can reinforce a territorial mentality, in which managers lock themselves in their functional fortresses and pull up the drawbridge, neglecting their responsibility to help their colleagues in other teams achieve college-wide goals.

Adopt a no-blame culture

People are less inclined to take the initiative and put their head over the parapet if they think their manager is perched in the next trench with a Gatling gun. Mistakes are opportunities for the individual and the whole organization to learn from. They are also inevitable. Repeatedly making the same error is obviously to be discouraged, but organizations that adopt a problem-solving and learning approach to failure are more likely to encourage people to be accountable for their actions and decisions.

Actively promote and enable self-development

One of the things we may want people to take more responsibility for is their own development. But this does not exonerate the college from ensuring the climate, funding and processes for this to happen. Asking people to take on more or different tasks than they have in the past requires us to equip them with the tools, skills and confidence to do so.

In short, accountability and improving performance need not be associated with purely transactional forms of management and close bureaucratic control. Might we actually create a greater sense of ownership by adopting some of the more involving and collaborative leadership strategies above?

A is for John Adair

John Adair, best-known for his book, *Effective Leadership*, first published in 1983, is one of the more eminent British writers on Leadership and Management.

His 'three circles' model presents leadership as being concerned with three interconnecting needs:

- the needs of the individual member of the team
- the needs of the team as a whole
- the demands of the task

In other words, successful leaders learn to balance these three elements in getting things done, ensuring that individuals are trained, appraised, given freedom to act, that the team is composed of the right people, properly briefed and encouraged to work together towards a common goal and that the task is properly understood and broken down into key objectives, with success measures and deadlines. These three overlapping circles form the basis of 'action-centred leadership'.

Each of the elements must be seen in relation to the other two, and if any one is neglected then the whole is undermined. So how might this apply to a manager in FE? Well, depending on your job, you may feel your influence over some of these areas is limited. However, even within the constrained role of, say, Section Leader, you can see how the three circles idea would apply: if you focus on hitting your targets at the expense of facilitating continuing professional development (CPD) for your team, then their motivation suffers, the team becomes dysfunctional and the task (i.e. targets) suffer. Similarly, if you nurture your team, but collectively lose sight of the task, then the team may lose direction and individuals will not have the opportunity to stretch themselves and grow.

Adair also examines leadership qualities, but again points out the power of balance, observing that over-application of noble qualities may be counter-productive. Honesty, perseverance and audacity, for example, can easily be pushed over into indiscretion, pig-headedness and irresponsible risk-taking.

You may like to read more about the way Adair uses this simple model to provide a wealth of instructive guidance on management tasks. You'll find his work listed in the References.

A is for Appraisal

What thoughts go through your mind when you see the title of this section? Excitement? Eager anticipation? Unbridled joy? Possibly not. Yet despite the efforts of many managers to get out of an annual task which they find as appealing as unblocking a drain, it is still likely these days in FE that you will be called upon to participate in formal appraisals, both as an appraiser and as an appraisee.

So why the sinking feeling? A number of explanations spring to mind:

- many of us have suffered at the hands of line managers or team leaders who do this badly
- we are all a little frightened about giving (and receiving) feedback
- for some, this is the only time that performance is discussed, and it therefore becomes a huge and daunting task
- we worry about our ability to control the conversation and the emotions it may release, particularly if we've been hearing rumours about performance-related pay
- it can feel like a confrontation and these are always easier to avoid than to face up to

Understandable though these feelings are, all of us like to know how we are getting on, what the organization and/or our own manager expects of us, and how we are going to learn and develop in our chosen career path. So, as managers, we may find ourselves laying claim to all sorts of alternative strategies:

- 'I speak to my staff every day, on an informal basis' (translation – 'I'm frightened of doing appraisals')

- 'I review targets on a regular basis at team meetings' (translation – 'I'm frightened of doing appraisals, but I like to crack the whip')
- 'My team are all experienced professionals. They know what they need to do' (translation – 'I won't take responsibility for being in charge, and I can't be bothered to agree objectives . . . Oh, and I'm frightened of doing appraisals')

Feeling more comfortable with the formal appraisal process requires three things:

- a clear understanding of why it's important
- the skills to handle the process competently and confidently
- an integrated approach to performance management, which sets the appraisal 'event' in a wider framework of management activity (see **P is for Performance Management**)

Since appraisal should be a two-way process, we can look at why it's important from two points of view:

The appraiser wants
- to reinforce good performance and positive behaviour on the part of the appraisee
- to identify and resolve jointly any problems in the appraisee's performance
- to agree objectives which
    - enable the appraisee to contribute fully to the future objectives of the college and the team
    - enable the appraisee to develop and grow appropriately in their role
- to leave the appraisee feeling motivated
- to improve or consolidate their relationship with the appraisee
- to get feedback on their own behaviour and performance

The appraisee wants
- to know where he/she stands, how they are doing
- to know how their contribution is valued
- to be congratulated where they have done well
- to find out what's coming up and what is expected of them

- to resolve any lingering frustrations in doing their job
- to agree how they can learn and develop

It's true that most of these outcomes can also be achieved through more frequent coaching sessions, provided these are regular and properly structured (see **M is for Mentoring and Coaching**). In this case, the annual appraisal can become more of an opportunity to take stock of the year, formally recognize achievements and agree long-term objectives and personal development plans. When performance is continuously monitored and discussed in this way, it immediately removes one of our earlier barriers to appraisal. It's no longer such a huge and daunting task. You may not be in a position to decide when and how formal appraisals are carried out, but you can choose to make these just one part of a staff development approach that also incorporates more frequent, coaching conversations.

So what skills do we need? In essence, they are the skills of any interview (see **I is for Interviews**), including rapport-building, listening, questioning, summarizing, etc. As with any interview, *preparation* by both parties is important.

As appraiser
- think about what the appraisee has done well/struggled with. Have examples.
- gather any necessary documentation (forms, booklet, guidance notes, last year's documents, evidence to support performance assessment).
- ensure you are familiar with any key standards (such as national standards for teaching in the Lifelong Learning Sector), the review process and/or appraisal scheme of the college (if there is one).
- consider the training and development needs of the appraisee.
- look at your objectives for the coming year and think about what the appraisee could do.
- seek views on the appraisee from colleagues and other appropriate people.
- agree a suitable time, date and venue (make adequate space. This is not a half-hour job and the meeting should not be interrupted.)

- think what might be on the the appraisee's agenda. Why not ask them?
- discuss all this with *your* manager.
- make sure the appraisee understands the appraisal process fully and check that they, too, have prepared.

As appraisee
- look at what you have achieved in the past year. Relate it to your objectives and to those of the team and college as a whole.
- what aspects of your job are you best at?
- consider what changes might help you do a better job (your skills/knowledge, your relationships, resources, responsibilities, etc. These will also include your CPD needs).
- are there any aspects of your role on which you need further clarification?
- are there other ways in which you could contribute to the team/college, and what support would you need to do this?
- do you have longer-term career plans? If so, what are they and how will you achieve them?

The approach to the actual appraisal discussion should be one of joint problem-solving and planning ('What can we do to help you develop and perform even better?'). The appraisee should do 70 per cent of the talking. In this respect it is very much a coaching dialogue (see **M is for Mentoring and Coaching**).

Other key skills needed for an effective appraisal discussion are giving and receiving feedback and jointly devising SMART (Specific, Measurable, Agreed, Realistic, Time-bound) objectives. You can read more about this in our sections **F is for Feedback** and **O is for Objectives**.

As for linking appraisal outcomes directly to pay, opinion in FE remains divided between those who see it as destructive, inhibiting open discussion and buy-in to self-development, and those who believe the financial incentive is vital to an integrated performance management approach. It's interesting to reflect, however, that at an organizational level the college itself is funded largely according to performance.

A is for Authenticity

The Principal of Bogginbrook College of FE is addressing staff at the start of the new academic year.

Colleagues, welcome. As I look around the team here, I can see quite a few different faces, and it's great to see new young staff coming in to replace some of the older experienced stagers we sadly had to say goodbye to last year.

I know we have embraced a lot of changes over the last year, and now, as we enter a new era in the development of Bogginbrook College of Further Education, we must build on these foundations to create a college fit for the twenty-first century. Here at Bogginbrook, we're all about creating added value for our students and the community at large. At the end of the day, it is our role to empower our learners, young and old, to contribute fully to UK plc, and enable us to compete more effectively and efficiently in an increasingly globalized economy.

Continuous improvement in quality standards is what will enable us to deliver on the challenges we are being set by government, and this means evaluating our performance on an ongoing basis to ensure that we are providing real value for money. As we continue on this journey of change, our staff are the most valuable resource an organization like ours has, so let us know your views. My senior colleagues and I have drawn up a vision and values statement for the college which we will be circulating shortly to seek your opinions. My door is always open . . .

Any of this have a familiar smell about it? The truth is such talk may mask genuinely noble intentions, but research indicates that people are generally disinclined to believe what senior managers tell them, at the best of times. To suggest that, aside from our immediate boss, we are always on the lookout for a charlatan with a hidden agenda is therefore not cynical, but merely realistic.

Building and maintaining the trust of your team is crucial to managers at all levels, and this is why many writers on the subject highlight authenticity or integrity as key components of successful leadership. But what is authenticity, and where does it come from? Here are some thoughts:

- It starts with self-awareness. Knowing yourself, being aware of your own strengths and shortcomings, and conscious of your emotional as well as intellectual responses helps you to be more sensitive to your impact on others. This is at the heart of Emotional Intelligence, which you can read more about in **E is for Emotional Intelligence**, and in Daniel Goleman's book, which you'll find in the References.

- Awareness of your own learning needs goes hand in hand with asking for feedback, admitting your mistakes and knowing when to ask for help.

- Understanding your own values enables you to acknowledge where these are compatible with those of the organization and where they are not.

- Honesty and sincerity are fundamental in building and maintaining trust. Yet, as a manager, you may not always feel that you can be open with information. If so, then be straight about what you can and cannot discuss. Respecting confidences, after all, is also a marker of integrity and trustworthiness.

- Hands up if you've ever worked with a very plausible manager who would say one thing to your face and then do another, intent on nothing so much as the advancement of their own career? As managers, we must do what we say we will do, and be seen to face up to bad news, while maintaining a positive focus on making things better.

- Some sort of ethical code to guide your decisions is vital when working in a rapidly changing environment, and often with incomplete information, as headline stories from the political and business world frequently remind us. Warren Bennis sees integrity as one of the four main competencies of leadership and talks about a 'moral compass' being the third leg of a tripod which leaders must keep in balance, (Bennis and Thomas 2002). The other two legs are ambition and competence. If any of these are too weak or too strong in relation to the others, then integrity is undermined (see **B is for Warren Bennis**).

- It may help to see trust as like Covey's 'emotional bank account' (Covey 1989). The more you deposit, by maintaining commitments, trusting others and treating people with respect and honesty, the more you are 'in credit', and likely to be trusted yourself, even if you occasionally let people down. However, managers who manipulate and dissemble, starving their teams of information and responsibility, will find their cheque bounces when they need extra effort and support.

B is for Benchmarking

Picture this. Harry and Sheena have just come out of a Section Heads meeting with the VP:

HARRY   Psst! Sheena! What was he going on about? What does he mean, 'benchmarking'?

SHEENA   Benchmarking. You know what benchmarking means. It's when you compare where you are – in terms of standards – with where you want to be. It's about identifying what needs to be improved, looking around to see where it's done better – inside or outside the college – and then implementing those same strategies to make improvements. So basically it's about raising standards and improving quality. It's also been called 'the art of stealing shamelessly'.

HARRY   But what's that got to do with benches, for goodness sake?

SHEENA   Oh, that's because of where the term comes from. It was originally about measuring productivity levels in industry. Management used to make a chalk mark on the work benches of those workers who were meeting the set targets, so other workers could follow their example.

HARRY   So if I arrive one morning and find the VP's chalked a big cross on my desk, I know I'm doing ok?

SHEENA   If that happened, Harry, I don't think it would be a good sign. Why don't you have a look at the LSDA 2002 publication on benchmarking in FE? It's in the college library.

Sheena could also have advised Harry to look on the LSDA website (lsda.org.uk) under publications. She has taken the 'stealing shamelessly' quote from Owen, J. (2002) *Benchmarking for the learning and skills sector*, LSDA.

B is for Warren Bennis

One of the twentieth century's foremost writers on leadership, Warren Bennis's work is mainly based on his many interviews with American leaders from industry, politics, academia and the voluntary sector. He has acted as advisor to four US presidents, and held a number of senior roles at academic institutions in the USA and elsewhere.

His writing frequently emphasizes the importance of self-awareness and self-knowledge in leadership, and the need for leaders to be true to themselves, rather than following standardized recipes of success. He is scathing about the tendency, as he sees it, to suppress, rather than encourage great leadership, and talks disparagingly of a generation of 'McLeaders'. He sees great leaders as being forged by a combination of the external circumstances of the time, their own personal qualities and the way in which they make meaning of their experiences. Although he often draws on individuals of great power and influence as examples, what he is saying is applicable to anyone in FE whose role involves leading people, whether that's on an institutional or team level.

The ability to adapt, to make meaning out of experience, which both yourself and your team can learn from, is a cornerstone of Bennis's view of leadership. It drives continuous learning and self-development, which are the hallmarks of successful leaders in every field and are processes eminently appropriate for the manager in FE.

Not surprisingly, generating trust by demonstrating integrity and candour is a vital function of leadership for Bennis, as is reflecting on experience for the purpose of developing yourself and mentoring others. He outlines four ways in which leaders can build and maintain trust:

- they are constant and avoid surprising their followers because they help them to make sense of what the external world throws at them
- they are consistent. They do what they say. Their actions match their words
- they are reliable, ensuring they are there to support their team, when needed
- they have integrity, and abide by their promises

But he also addresses the importance of creating a clear vision, 'managing the dream', of engaging and motivating others through constant communication, and of having a bias towards action and results, which includes taking appropriate risks. In your role as an FE manager, it may well not be within your remit to create either the dream or the vision for the institution as a whole. These things are normally generated at the most senior level, or even imposed from outside the institution – for example, by government departments. But you can manage and mediate them for your team; and you can create and sustain a team or department-specific vision, a sense of purpose and identity which includes but goes deeper and wider than the meeting of externally imposed targets.

It's not possible to do justice to all of Bennis's ideas here, and we have addressed elsewhere (see **L is for Leadership**) his contribution to the debate on leadership versus management, but you can read more of his thoughts on these topics in some of the books mentioned in our Reference section at the end of the book, notably *On Becoming a Leader*.

B is for Bullying

As an FE manager you have a threefold responsibility with regard to the bullying of staff by other staff: how to spot it; how to stop it; and how to avoid doing it yourself or having it done to you.

Let's look first at how to spot it. Which of the following incidents, if any, would you say constitutes bullying as defined by your college's anti-bullying policy?

(i)   JASON   Parveen, I need those retention and achievement figures right now.

     PARVEEN   I know. Sorry. They're not quite . . .

     JASON   You've had plenty of time to get them in. I need them now.

     PARVEEN   The trouble is, there's been so much paperwork . . .

     JASON   I don't want any more lame excuses. They told me you were useless when I first came here, and I can see they were right.

(ii)   NORMAN   Evening.

     ZOË   Oh! Blimey, you scared me, there. I thought I was the only one left in the building.

     NORMAN   I like to see my team working late. Now, I understand you've made a complaint to the VP about the recruitment of students in this School.

     ZOË   Er . . .

     NORMAN   I'm not quite sure why you went over my head, Zoë.

     ZOË   I didn't. I talked to you about it, and you said there was nothing you could do. And the thing is, Norman, we're recruiting kids onto the programme who just can't cope with the work. It's creating horrendous problems for the teaching team as well as for the learners . . .

NORMAN   My advice to you, my dear, is don't rock the boat. It won't be good for your career prospects.

(iii) SHEENA   My desk is broken. Could I have a new one?
PARVEEN   As Head of Section I have to say no.
SHEENA   But everyone else has just had a new one.
PARVEEN   Nothing left in the budget.
SHEENA   Well, could I have a three-drawer filing cabinet? I've been struggling since I came here, storing everything in a couple of cardboard boxes. Everybody else has got a filing cabinet.
PARVEEN   No. Nothing left in the budget.
SHEENA   What about a key to the staff toilet? I still haven't got one. I'm the only one who hasn't.
PARVEEN   No. Sorry. Budget.
SHEENA   Couple of ballpoint pens?
PARVEEN   No. Sorry.

You are likely to find that your college's anti-bullying policy would identify all of these interactions as examples of bullying. In (i) Jason is perfectly within his rights as manager to chase Parveen for the R&A returns. Where he oversteps the mark is in his final remark where he insults and undermines her. Even if what he says is factually accurate here, his communicating it in this way and in this context constitutes bullying. In (ii) it is not the fact that Norman confronts Zoë with what she has done, but rather that he lurks about after dark to catch her on her own and issue a veiled threat that defines this as bullying behaviour. In example (iii) the problem is not that Parveen says she can't afford to provide Sheena with necessary resources, but that she has managed to provide them for everyone else and is therefore discriminating against this one member of the School.

Bullying and harassment are often used interchangeably, with some organizations defining bullying as a form of harassment. Your college may have its own definition, but here is ours:

Harassment is any behaviour (such as statements or actions) which is based on any social factor and is offensive to any recipient. 'Social factor' includes race, culture, nationality, ethnicity, religion, gender, sexuality, disability, age, marital status, physical trait or social status. 'Any recipient' will include any person who witnesses the behaviour as well as the person to whom the behaviour is directed.

In terms of how to stop bullying, it is essential that college procedures are followed scrupulously. Failure to do so can compromise the fairness of the ensuing process as well as the legal position of the college and the individuals involved. As an employer, the college is responsible for preventing bullying and harassment, which can lead to low morale, stress, increased sickness absence, poor employee relations and the loss of talented people. It may also find itself taken to an employment tribunal answering claims of discrimination (see **E is for Equal Opportunities**). As a manager, you should refer all alleged cases of staff bullying to the college's HR manager so that matters are investigated properly and correct procedures followed. It is rarely advisable for you to intervene, beyond an initial word with the parties involved to see whether a resolution can be reached informally before referring the matter on. Cases of alleged bullying should always be taken seriously; but unfortunately they are notoriously difficult to prove.

As for the methods to avoid inadvertently being a bully yourself or being subjected to bullying, make sure you are familiar with your college's policy. As well as threats, insults and discrimination, bullying behaviour can include shouting, swearing, excluding or marginalizing, spreading malicious rumours, ridiculing or demeaning, repeated unconstructive criticism or unwelcome sexual advances. Obviously all of these behaviours are not only to be avoided yourself but also treated with **zero tolerance** within your team.

If you want to read more about what bullying is and how else it might manifest itself, take a look at the ACAS website (accessed on 14/3/2006):

www.acas.org.uk/index.aspx?articleid=797

C is for Change

Think back five years, or maybe just twelve months. How much has changed about your college, management structures, curriculum requirements, standards and targets, your job and what is expected of you? If the answer is not much, you probably don't work in Further Education and you've accidentally picked up the wrong book. Perhaps you've landed recently from outer space, or been defrosted from some glacier in the Dolomites, complete with flint axe and a slightly puzzled expression.

Organizations everywhere, inside and outside of the education sector, are experiencing continual change. The pace may vary, but the change never stops, and managers at all levels play a key role in helping their teams and their institutions respond successfully to what can sometimes seem like unmanageable chaos (and sometimes it doesn't just *seem* that way . . .).

Let's take just one small-scale example. At Bogginbrook College of Further Education, falling demand for programmes in Secretarial and Receptionist skills has led to the decision to merge the Office Arts section with the Business Studies section to create a School of Business. To examine the issues at stake, we will use a framework for change, which incorporates ideas from a number of eminent thinkers on the topic, including Barrett (1998), Bridges (1991), Kotter (1996), Schein (1992) and Senge (1990).

Now, have a look at the diagram below:

How can managers take account of each of these aspects of the change process in order to ensure that objectives are met and they bring people along with them as well?

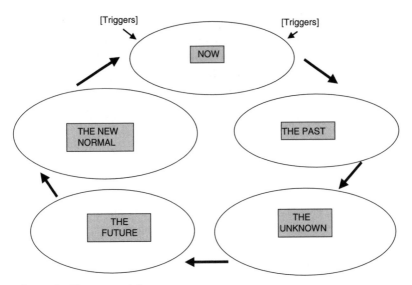

Figure 1 Change model

Now

Change is usually the result of some combination of internal and/or external triggers. For example, a deterioration in our health or nagging from our friends or family may induce us to try to stop smoking. In the case of Bogginbrook College, falling student rolls have combined with financial pressures to raise questions about the viability of certain programmes and the departments which were built around them. Whatever the trigger, successful change generally starts with an understanding of where we are now and why.

This means listening to different accounts, or 'stories', in order to appreciate where different interest groups may be coming from, and what the strengths of the current state of affairs are, not just the weaknesses. Before rushing in to change anything, the senior managers at Bogginbrook must be sure that they have understood the reasoning behind the current departmental structure, what worked well about it, and how different groups of staff view the current challenge. They will then be better placed to anticipate the concerns of staff and the likely sources of resistance to change.

The past

Aside from failing to understand the present situation fully, one of the most common mistakes managers make when faced with change is to 'trash the past'. How often have you seen eager 'new brooms' come into an organization (or indeed sector), only to criticize and sweep away all that has gone before, regardless of merit, in the cause of justifying their appointment?

If the Bogginbrook managers are shrewd, they will build a vision of what is over and done with and what is not, and communicate this clearly to staff, while at the same time showing respect for what has been achieved in the past. They will be unambiguous about what must change, but support people and help them to adjust their 'mental models' to cope with the new reality.

The unknown

If life were easy and change predictable and under our control, we would move seamlessly from old state to new state, just as we had planned it, with the grateful cheers of the college's staff ringing in our ears. Of course, what actually happens is we shove off from a safe and familiar harbour, expecting to discover the East Indies, and end up in an entirely new continent. Not only that, but in the meantime we have to cope with weeks or months of not knowing where the hell we are, or whether we will get anywhere at all.

Successful managers at every level prepare people for this uncertainty (even when they may be experiencing it themselves) and help them to cope with it by encouraging experimentation and new ideas. They accept the learning that failure brings. They use short-term action planning and review, so that people can see progress, however slight, and feel confident that change is happening. Most of all, they make themselves visible (see **W is for Walking Around**), and they over-communicate to ensure that no one feels isolated and consensus is reinforced.

The future

Let's imagine that at Bogginbrook the structural changes have now been achieved, roles have been changed and those whose jobs were lost have gone. The combined school is now in place and looks something like what was originally planned. As the future takes shape, the managers make a point of reminding people of that vision, the purpose behind the changes and what they were designed to achieve.

They also review success measures in order to celebrate early successes and try to prioritize actions, which will bring about 'quick wins'. In helping colleagues adjust to this new future, they do not exclusively focus on processes, systems and structures, but engage people in establishing the culture and values of the new school, appealing to hearts as well as minds by painting a compelling picture of all it will achieve.

The new normal

Anyone who has made a New Year's resolution understands the fragility of change and how good intentions slip back into old behaviours so easily when the pressure is on. Working in a new way once or twice does not guarantee permanent change.

For Bogginbrook to really embed the changes in its new school, it must continue to monitor performance and reinforce new approaches. It must ensure that knock-on effects to other schools and departments are managed, and policies and strategies altered where necessary to integrate the new structure. It must recognize the difference between grudging compliance and a genuine behaviour change, which stems from new learning and a shift in underlying assumptions about the way things should work.

Ultimately, change will only truly be embedded when people don't just do things differently, but feel and think differently too. It is an emotional journey for each individual, as well as a rational one, with all of the uncertainties and unpredictability that that implies. Understanding this is a good start to recognizing what you can and cannot control, as a manager, and accepting that, to be successful and lasting, change must gain acceptance and not simply be imposed.

Here's that diagram again (see page 28), this time summarizing the key factors that come into play when we engage in institutional change.

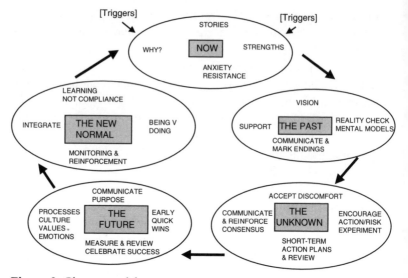

Figure 2 Change model

C is for the Cinderella sector

Ever wondered where this overused metaphor came from? Well, it was Kenneth Baker, in his role as Secretary of State for Education under Margaret Thatcher back in the 1980s, who described FE as a Cinderella – always undervalued and under-funded. This seemed to hold out a promise of better times to come, of course, when Cinderella would actually get to go to the Ball. It also, rather bizarrely, appeared to cast Schools and Higher Education in the role of ugly sisters; although – strange to say – you'll rarely hear either of them referred to as the Ugly Sister sector.

So what does this suggest for your role, as a manager? Are you Buttons, or the Fairy Godmother, or the Handsome Prince? Gender aside, you'll probably find yourself, at one time or another, enacting all of these. As Buttons you can be the sympathetic colleague, who can empathize and sympathize, have a chat, have a joke, be approachable. As the Fairy Godmother you can act as mentor, or make things happen, or put things right. The problematic side of this role, of course, is that you may be expected to solve every problem with a wave of your wand. You may even have that expectation of yourself, which is just asking for trouble. As the Handsome Prince you may find yourself in a position to promote and demote (though hopefully not on the basis of people's shoe size). You will certainly find yourself in a high-profile position where your decisions and conduct have the potential to win or lose you the respect of those you manage. Above all, you will be in a position to do something – however small – to enhance the reputation of FE and raise its profile and its status.

C is for Consult or Control

This section briefly addresses one key aspect of leadership, which is the question of 'command and control' versus more consultative and involving styles. What is the 'right' amount of freedom to give people, in order to motivate and develop them? Does control make for efficient management and higher quality standards, or does it merely stifle creativity and erode the initiative and energy of your best people? Some sections in this book (see **C is for Change, D is for Delegation, M is for Mentoring and Coaching**) may seem to favour freedom, while others (**D is for Disciplinary, M is for Meetings, O is for Objectives**) contain more elements of control and standardization.

You may feel that there is a place for both control and individual initiative, and indeed, effective leaders tend to find their own balance between these extremes. They adjust this balance depending on the circumstances and the individual person they are dealing with. This contingency approach has been written about by various people, but perhaps made most accessible by Ken Blanchard (Blanchard *et al.* 1986), he of the 'One Minute Manager' books. You can find references in our suggested reading.

In his model, the leadership approach is defined by the degree of direction given (high or low) and the degree of support given (high or low). This gives four broad categories, or leadership styles, which the leader may move between according to the demands of the situation and the individual:

Directive: high degree of direction, but low support. In other words, the leader gives detailed instructions, which are not for debate, and expects them to be followed.

Coaching: high degree of direction and lots of support too. So the leader still tells people the task and the way to do it, but also offers to help and coach the person in achieving it. (Do not confuse this convenient label with coaching itself, which may, like leadership, be more or less directive.)

Supporting: low levels of direction, but highly supportive. Here, the leader trusts the person's ability to achieve the task with little direction as to how, but they are ready to jump in and provide additional help if problems of commitment or motivation arise.

Delegating: low in both direction and support. The leader places enough confidence in someone's experience and reliability to simply 'agree and forget'. Given a clear objective, they are confident the person will deliver without any interference from them.

Having established this outline, we can probably all think of times in our lives when we've been on the receiving end of each of these styles of leadership, and no doubt we will recall some of them more fondly than others, depending on how appropriately they were used. Try matching the following examples to what you think is the appropriate style.

Sheena has many years' experience at the college and knows the local area well. She is actually very capable, but her confidence has taken a hammering, due to a history of bullying by overbearing bosses. You want her to take on liaison with secondary schools in your vicinity.

Zöe, a bright and enthusiastic new member of staff, has just joined your Faculty from another college, and this is her first management role. You are helping her to organize her first major field trip for students.

Kimberley, the highly efficient School secretary, has worked at the college just about longer than any other member of staff. She is renowned for her annual organization of the Staff Barbecue, which has developed over the years into quite an event. You want her to sort out this year's 'do'.

Harry is relatively new to the role of Section Leader, and you suspect he may have been over-promoted. He does not always make a priority of what he sees as 'extra-curricular' tasks and struggles to keep up to speed with the rapidly changing FE environment. You think a change of scene might help test his mettle, and arrange for him to lead a new adult numeracy programme, something he has not done before.

What's your view? Here's ours: Sheena will probably require Supporting, since she knows what needs to be done, it is just a question of the confidence to do it. Zöe is highly motivated, but inexperienced and unfamiliar with her new environment. The safety risk is high, so it is best to adopt a Directive style at first.

Kimberley clearly knows what she is doing and relishes her task. A Delegating style should be safe to use here. Finally, Harry is not only unfamiliar with his new task, but may be inclined to give it a low priority. He will probably need the high direction and support of a Coaching approach.

In reality, of course, there are many more subtleties of leadership style than our simple summary would suggest. Assuming there is always one right answer may be seen as somewhat naïve. But this kind of model at least encourages us to be flexible and consider the needs of the individual team member, as well as helping us to think about how we might employ different approaches in different circumstances.

D is for Delegation

Delegation is a term which is bandied about more often than it is understood.

When a manager delegates, they should be giving someone else the *authority*, responsibility and *initiative* to perform some *agreed* task. The key words here are the ones in italics, because they are usually the first ones to be forgotten by poor delegators. What they do is try to dump all the responsibility onto you, whether you want it or not, and give you no additional authority or help. This is just abdication. Worse still, is when they do this and then constantly stick their nose in and interfere, because 'you're not doing it right'.

Good delegation implies that the manager retains some overall control, and checks on the performance of their team member. It also implies that both parties are willing for this responsibility to be re-assigned.

Of course, if it all goes pear-shaped, you, the manager, cannot escape responsibility, even though you have delegated the task. It is your fault because you've delegated badly. It's tough at the top.

Having said that, delegation brings all sorts of benefits:

- it helps you improve your use of time
- it makes the team more flexible by encouraging shared tasks and know-how
- it motivates your team
- it helps to grow and develop your team members
- it therefore leads to more potential successors

So what stops us from delegating properly?

(a) it leads to more potential successors
(b) we're frightened of losing control
(c) the team member is not properly trained to carry out the task

(d) we like to stick with old jobs we know we're good at
(e) we tend to think only we can do the job 'properly' (i.e. in the same way)
(f) the task is not really suitable, perhaps for confidential reasons
(g) we cannot be bothered to explain a task to someone else
(h) it makes us feel secure to do something our team can't
(i) the task is too urgent for us to have time to brief someone else properly

If you are thinking that some of these reasons sound better than others, you are right. Which do you think are the acceptable reasons not to delegate? (See our view at the end of this section.)

Nevertheless, by following a few simple guidelines, effective delegation can be within every manager's grasp:

- ensure you fully understand the purpose and contribution of *your* job
- identify *your* priority objectives and how your team can contribute to these
- think which tasks may be suited to delegation
- ensure you understand the strengths, future potential and current workload of each of your team. Do not put individuals under undue stress
- decide what should be delegated, who can handle it and benefit from it, and whether any additional training is needed
- agree SMART objectives, including precise timescales and ensure limits of authority are understood (see **O is for Objectives**)
- agree how performance will be monitored
- make sure other relevant people know what you've done
- allow the team member to take the initiative, but be available to help
- give constructive feedback and allow people to take the credit

Will things go wrong occasionally? Will people let you down? Well yes, obviously. Delegation will always be a calculated risk. But bear in mind that there is nothing that reflects better on a manager than growing a team of able people and potential successors, who continually get the chance to impress others with what they can do.

(We would only see c), f) and i) as valid reasons not to delegate.)

D is for Disciplinary

A number of complaints have been made over the last year against Angela. She has taught at Bogginbrook College for 28 years. She's a section leader in Norman's School, and the start of the complaints has coincided with her being given responsibility – against her express wishes – for coordinating the 14–16 provision within the School. This role carries no enhancement in terms of salary or promotion. The complaints are:

- She's been consistently late for her classes and has, on seven occasions, not turned up for a scheduled class at all. (source of complaint: students)
- She's been absent from college on two occasions for over a week without notifying Norman, her manager, or making arrangements for her classes or management duties to be covered. (source of complaint: Norman, her Head of School)
- She has completed no attendance registers – neither hard copy nor electronic – for three terms, nor completed last term's Retention and Achievement returns. (source of complaint: Norman, her Head of School)
- She has spoken disparagingly about – and directly to – the 14–16 year-old students, referring to them as 'Babbies', 'No-hopers' and 'Losers'. (source of complaint: parents and students)
- The achievement and retention figures for her section are very poor and two recent college Self Assessment reports found her teaching to be 'unsatisfactory'.

This is what her Head of School, Norman, has to say:

Angela doesn't seem willing to address any of these issues, and is particularly defensive about her teaching being criticized. And I'm not happy about

her response to the paperwork issues and her unauthorized absence. I've told
her I'm not satisfied, and I've arranged a meeting for next Wednesday so I
can let her know what the next steps will be.

Now, whatever we may think of Norman and his management style, we need to look at this case dispassionately in order to judge whether disciplinary action is appropriate. Disciplinary action may be taken against a member of staff for a range of reasons. There may have been misconduct of some kind, or the member of staff's performance may be in question. In Angela's case it seems to be a matter of both. If the complaints had only concerned her performance in teaching and supporting learning, the first resort could have been to employ informal methods (such as CPD, or **Mentoring and Coaching**) to improve her performance. If this proved ineffective, only then would disciplinary action become inevitable. And of course it's essential to remember that the purpose of disciplinary action, too, is to improve performance. But we must also bear in mind that the final sanction for management – if no improvement is evident – is the power to dismiss.

In case you, as line manager, should need to instigate, or should become caught up in, a disciplinary process involving one of your team, you will need to make yourself familiar – if you are not already – with your College Disciplinary Policy and Procedure. It's also important that you understand and bear in mind the constraints under which the college management operates and particularly the broad legal framework which protects an employee against unfair or constructive dismissal. Certain elements of best practice have now been enshrined in law, in the form of a statutory minimum procedure applying to action which may lead to dismissal. These obligatory elements are:

- informing someone in writing of any allegations against them
- holding a meeting with the person concerned to discuss any allegations, hear their account and decide what action should be taken
- allowing the individual to be accompanied at this meeting if they wish
- giving the individual the right of appeal against the action decided upon

Your own college policy will include this and more, but you can also find helpful advice on the ACAS website (accessed 25 April 2006): www.acas.org.uk/index.aspx?articleid=906

A useful text is Torrington *et al.* (2001), chapter 13 which covers issues of discipline and dismissal.

D is for Peter Drucker

Born in Vienna, but spending most of his working life in the US, Peter Drucker is well known to business studies students as one of the most influential management thinkers of the last century. Although largely associated in people's minds with big business, holding professorial posts at New York University and Claremont Graduate School in California, Drucker firmly believed that management was not just something for business, and that the private sector could learn much in this area from non-profit organizations. He believed that *every* organization should be based on learning and teaching.

He coined the term 'knowledge workers', and wrote extensively about the impact on management and society at large of manual workers being replaced by this new breed of employee. 'Knowledge workers', as the name suggests, bring knowledge to the enterprise, rather than manual skills. They produce ideas and information and decisions, rather than 'things', and must often know more than their bosses about the specific job in hand. Managing these sorts of teams means enabling them to perform together, by agreeing goals, common values, appropriate structures, and by supporting personal development.

Whereas large manual workforces of old were kept away from decisions by mass production technologies and 'scientific management', 'knowledge workers' necessitate the extension of decision-making to more and more staff. The job of managers becomes increasingly to make people effective (ensure they *do the right things*), not just efficient (ensuring they *do things right*). Thus, Drucker sees management by control, whether directly or via restrictive procedures and reporting, as counter-productive, and management by objectives as a more appropriate way to motivate staff. According to him, the ingredients of a successfully managed enterprise are therefore:

- common goals and shared values
- clear, open communication and individual responsibility
- productive relationships, teamwork and self-development
- built-in performance mechanisms through measurement and continuous improvement
- a recognition that results can only be external (educated students, healed patients, satisfied customers). Everything internal is a cost
- a focus on *contribution*, so that people agree what they contribute to the organization, but also know what colleagues need from them in order to make their own contribution

These conditions enable management by 'self-control'.

Drucker also takes a pragmatic approach to leadership, rejecting the idea of charismatic leadership in favour of leadership as hard work, as the sometimes tedious business of getting goals and priorities properly thrashed out and ensuring people understand. Leadership is about accepting responsibility, earning trust and matching words with deeds. It is more about being consistent than being clever. Drucker finds no correlation between intelligence or creativity and effectiveness. Effectiveness is a discipline to be learned like any other.

E is for Emotional Intelligence

Where your own Christmas email to your section might say:

Thanks to all of you for all your hard work this term. I hope those of you who are able to spare the time will join me in 001 for mince pies and cheese this lunchtime.

Norman's might read:

I remind colleagues that the College does not officially finish until 5pm this evening. CCTV cameras in the car park will record anyone leaving early.

This may be because Norman is not very emotionally intelligent.

It has become quite fashionable to talk about different intelligences. And, however you define them, it's likely that, as a manager in FE, you've found you're going to need every single one of them. Emotional intelligence is a term popularized by Goleman (1996). It means, among very many other things, the ability to read how others are feeling; the ability to imagine yourself in someone else's shoes. The intelligence to speak and act in a way that takes account of how others may be feeling is clearly a useful (though arguably not yet sufficiently widespread) management skill. An emotionally intelligent manager will typically be one who builds up people's self-esteem, treats them with respect, consults (where possible) rather than dictates. They should never be confused with a 'soft' or non-assertive manager. Indeed, they may, like Shackleton, for example, have a quite directive style. But what their emotional intelligence will provide above all is the ability to build and motivate effective teams.

How is this achieved? It begins with being aware of your own emotions and how they may impact upon your judgement or behaviour at any given time. This aspect of emotional intelligence is too often overlooked, a too common assumption being that to demonstrate emotional intelligence we have to be warm and cuddly or do a lot of crying in public. This isn't at all what emotional intelligence is about. Developing a greater awareness of your own emotional responses to people and situations enables you to take a step back and reflect before you act. Is your colleague Norman really a poor manager, for example, or is it just that you find his style antithetical and irritating? Is Angela's performance really giving cause for concern, or is your unease about her partly because she reminds you of your Auntie Joan who scared the pants off you?

Emotional intelligence, then, is about recognizing and addressing the fact that your own emotions may influence your attitudes and behaviour; and at the same time recognizing the emotional impact your behaviour may have on others.

For the record, you're probably right to be concerned about Norman (see **B is for Bullying**) and Angela (see **D is for Disciplinary**), though it's to be hoped that someone with sufficient emotional intelligence further up the line of management might spot a link between the two sets of behaviours and treat it as a wider management problem.

E is for Equal Opportunities

You have, of course, like any good manager, familiarized yourself with your college's Equal Opportunities policy. As with the Anti-Bullying policy, you'll need a working knowledge of the current regulations and required procedures in case you are called upon to respond to incidents or allegations which fall under the categories covered by the policy. There are also background issues about Equal Opportunities in FE, however, of which you need to remain mindful.

The traditional profile of managers, particularly senior managers, in the FE sector has been predominantly white and male. While the same is true of other organizations and institutions, the pattern persisted in FE longer than might have been hoped. This has resulted in it being a recurring issue on the agenda of national bodies such as LSC and Ofsted and has led to initiatives such as the LSC's undertaking to the Commission for Black Staff in FE to encourage and support FE colleges in modelling best race equality practice as employers.

On an individual scale, for yourself as a manager, it presents a number of challenges. If you are a woman and/or non-white, these may be personal and professional ones about career trajectory and progression. But for all managers, there may well be issues to address about role modelling. If you work in a college where managers are predominantly white or predominantly male, or, for example, include none with a disability, or where that pattern is evident in the most senior positions, you will need to consider the possible effects on the career aspirations of those members of your team who may see themselves as marginalized in relation to the dominant groups. And although race and gender are the current high-profile issues of concern in relation to equal opportunities for FE managers, the same principle applies where management or senior management teams are seen as predominantly or exclusively able-bodied, heterosexual, under 40 or over 50. The thing to remember is that, despite the best intentions of a college's Equal Opportunities Policy, inequality of opportunity can nevertheless appear implicit in an organization where members of particular groups are never or rarely seen in management or senior management positions. It can lead to talented people leaving the college on the assumption that they'll get nowhere if they stay.

At a programme leader and team leader level, it can also have a critical impact on student recruitment, retention and achievement, for example in curriculum areas which were traditionally thought of as gender-specific (such as Nursery Nursing or Trowel Trades). An all-male teaching team and hierarchy in the Engineering section could be a factor in discouraging the recruitment of women learners, or contributing to low retention rates (or low achievement rates) among women learners. And the converse is equally possible in a Health and Social Care School with an exclusively female staffing profile. With the current emphasis on targets, such issues need some consideration.

The extent to which you can address any of this directly will depend on your position and seniority within the college. At the very least, as a first-line manager leading a small team, you can ensure that those whom you manage (and those whom they teach) feel valued as individuals and – if necessary – are exposed to a diverse and balanced range of role models, for example through mentoring arrangements, visits, continuing professional development programmes and contacts with outside bodies.

F is for Feedback

A key skill in **mentoring, coaching** and performance **appraisal** and **interview** follow-up is giving feedback, an activity most of us approach with some trepidation. What often happens is that we criticize, our appraisee gets defensive, so we justify ourselves, so our appraisee switches off, and the whole exercise ends in failure. Or we lavish undeserved praise on them because it's easier that way and nice to make somebody smile; but of course this gets us absolutely nowhere either in terms of our targets or the appraisee's development or performance. So here are some helpful hints on how to avoid these pitfalls:

When giving feedback:

- be *prompt*, whether it is positive or negative.
- create the right *conditions*. Feedback should take place in an atmosphere of trust and real rapport.
- ask *questions* to enable them to assess themselves first.
- begin with 2 or 3 *positive things* which you want to praise.
- follow with something that would make the performance even better next time.
- be *specific and objective* – give examples and reasons.
- don't be afraid to discuss how it makes you or them *feel* – good or bad.
- be clear about what the *consequences* of not improving their performance are.
- recognize what contribution you may have made to any problems.
- make clear your positive desire to *help resolve* any problems.
- ask for *their response* to what you have said.
- finish with an *overall positive comment*. Consider getting them to summarize.

(adapted from Wallace and Gravells 2005)

F is for Foster Report

The report on the Foster Review of Further Education was published in November 2005. It is one example of the wide range of reports, reviews, consultations and **White Papers** whose recommendations, analyses or directives have a successive (and sometimes, it seems, all too frequent) impact on your working life as an FE manager. In the case of the Foster Report it is perhaps the *vision* put forward of FE – as a cornerstone of the Skills Sector – which should give you, with your manager's hat on, most pause for thought. After all, many working in FE – and this may include yourself – may not share exactly this vision of what it is they're about. It simply may not coincide with their own perception of their purpose, their identity or their role. For example, you may have people on your team whose motivation to teach in FE is driven by their belief in education for the sake of the individual rather than in skills training for the sake of the economy. There is always a danger with *visions* that they may not be unanimously shared. Not everyone may buy into them; and this is particularly a risk when the vision appears to be imposed from above or – as in this case – from outside the college altogether. What this means in practical management terms is that you will have to manage the vision (see **B is for Warren Bennis**) in order to safeguard against some of those you manage losing motivation or the will to cooperate. One of the requirements of an effective manager is the ability to navigate through the squalls caused by philosophical and political positionings such as these, steering in the required direction while maintaining a 'happy ship' in which everyone's right to a point of view is valued. This needs more than **emotional intelligence**; it requires you to see things coming. And that in turn means keeping updated by familiarizing yourself with the contents of the Reviews, Reports and **White Papers** pertaining to the Learning and Skills sector as and when they appear (see **U is for Updating**).

It's interesting to note that Foster describes FE not as a **Cinderella**, but as a **'Middle Child'**. This alternative metaphor may be a useful one to you as manager in motivating those you manage. It is presumably intended to position the sector between schools (youngest child) and HE (oldest) while pointing out that it is often, undeservedly, neglected in favour of the other two. Well, at least it gets us out of the realms of pantomime.

F is for Funding

There is a sense in which we could say that the issue of Funding underpins every other aspect of the FE manager's role. As we write, the key source of funding for FE provision is the Learning and Skills Council (LSC); but whatever changes may come about – and in FE we can always count on change – two aspects of funding are likely to remain constant. These are:

- the need to balance Value for Money on one hand with attention to Quality on the other
- the link between funding and the retention and achievement of learners

Let's now unpack each of these in turn in the context of the funding mechanisms currently in place, and identify some of the dilemmas facing managers in FE at every level.

Creating a balance between Value for Money and Quality of provision

In terms of funding there are currently two types of course: Listed and Load-banded.

1   Listed courses receive a guaranteed amount of funding, whatever the hours given to class contact. The decision about the number of contact hours will be taken on the basis of:

- guidelines from the awarding body
- the need to keep costs down as far as is consistent with . . .
- . . . issues about the quality of the provision

Within these three criteria, the manager will have only limited room to manoeuvre. One of the ways to keep costs down, for example, is to opt for large class sizes. But, with a very high ratio of learners to teacher, some degree of individual teacher–learner contact is inevitably lost, and this in turn has an impact on the quality of provision.

2   Load-banded courses are funded according to the 'band' their hours fall within. So, to take a fictional example, imagine there was a band of up to 30 hours which attracted a certain sum of funding, and that the next band, attracting a higher sum, was for courses of between 31 and 40 hours, then the prudent manager could well take the decision to allocate 31 hours to the course. This would represent the absolute minimum number of hours needed to place the course in the higher funded band. Again, however, there would be the need to perform a balancing act with the key criteria when making the final decisions about the hours to be allocated, in terms of:

- guidelines from the awarding body and
- locating the course within the optimum possible band for funding, while
- ensuring that hours don't fall below what is required to sustain quality of provision.

The link between funding and the retention and achievement of learners

For FE managers (and, it could well be argued, for teachers too) Retention and Achievement are terms of enormous significance. As we write, 10 per cent of the funding from the LSC is dependent on student achievement. Funding is paid to the college in tranches at fixed dates during the year; and returns must be made in preparation for each of these, detailing numbers of learners enrolled on each course and, where appropriate – following summative assessment for example – figures for learner achievement in terms of successful completion (see **P is for Paperwork**). Clearly the correlation between numbers enrolled and numbers successfully completing is going to be key here in securing the optimum funding. The astute manager, therefore, will be well advised to:

- Keep a close eye on learner recruitment to ensure that

learners who are enrolled on a course possess the necessary skills and knowledge to cope with its demands, and the necessary motivation to stay the course (literally!). Of course, this involves some element of selection. But it's selection for a course or programme rather than selection for entry to the institution itself. An FE college will usually have a sufficiently broad curriculum to accommodate most learners' needs. A manager who is keeping a close eye on funding will see it as good sense to match the learner carefully to the course that best suits that learner's needs.

- Monitor learner progress with great care in the initial week or so of the course, so that learners who are unlikely to complete successfully can be identified early and enrolled on a programme more compatible with their needs. This is not just in the learner's best interests, but is absolutely crucial in terms of funding since once a learner counts as enrolled, their subsequent failure to successfully complete – whether because they later leave the course or stay but fail to achieve their qualification – means a loss of funding.

In other words, lost learners translate into lost money, and learner success translates into value for money for the college.

For the Team Leader or Section Leader or Head of School it is essential, therefore, to focus on careful management of the following three elements which are inextricably linked:

- funding
- selection of learners for courses
- quality of teaching and learning

If the quality of teaching is poor or inadequate this will have a knock-on effect on student retention and achievement, which in turn will have a knock-on effect on funding. Similarly, if funding restraints lead to the necessity for large class sizes or reduced hours or both, the resulting loss of teacher–learner contact time may have a negative impact on the quality of provision and lead to poor retention and achievement rates, which in turn lead to a further loss of funding. It's this sort of vicious circle which the FE manager has to do their best to avoid, and why achieving the balance between Quality and Value for Money is so crucial to their role.

The LSC and plan-led funding

The other key aspect of funding which has an impact on managers' scope for action and decision-making is in relation to curriculum provision. Put simply, the LSC steers the FE college's curriculum provision through its plan-led funding. As we write, the key areas for funding are dictated by government targets in relation to:

- full-time 16–19 year olds
- Basic Skills training
- Level 2 entitlement (aimed to provide every adult with a minimum Level 2 qualification)
- Level 3 'Jumpers' – those adults entitled to Level 2 but proceeding straight to a Level 3 qualification

These are nominated priority areas. Funding for non-priority areas, such as Adult Education, is diminishing as LSC resourcing is increasingly focused on those designated target areas. Courses in non-priority areas can often only run if learners are prepared to pay substantial fees. So, in terms of curriculum planning, the manager will be constrained by these two factors:

(a) how to optimize provision which falls within plan-led funding
(b) what the market will bear in terms of fees for provision in non-priority, full-cost areas

The implications of plan-led funding clearly extend into all areas of the manager's role. To take **Human Resources** as an example, there will be a need to match teacher expertise to the requirements of the target courses; and so you may be faced with the necessity of moving established teachers out of their comfort zone in order to undertake professional development which will enable them to contribute to programmes they were not initially employed to teach (for example, provision for 14–16 year olds). Or, for teachers in non-priority areas, you may be faced with the difficult issues of redundancy or early retirement.

As an FE manager, then, Funding is an issue which affects almost every decision you make; and almost every decision you make will have an effect on Funding. To maintain clarity of purpose, you need to remember this mantra:

*Quality of Provision + Value for Money = Successful Curriculum
Management*

Useful links

You'll find website addresses in the References section for

1   the Learning Aims Database (awarding body recommenda-
    tions on guided learning hours)
2   The LSC Funding Guide

G is for Getting Organized

Harry has recently been given responsibility for leading the Numeracy strand of the college's Skills for Adult Learners initiative. He still has a classroom teaching workload, albeit reduced, and he is studying part-time for his Master's in Education. Here he is taking a few messages from Kimberley, the School secretary.

KIMBERLEY   Don't rush off, Harry. There've been a few phone messages for you. I don't know why they've come through to me. Is your voicemail switched on?

HARRY   Yes, but I've not checked it recently. Well, not since last Monday actually. Oh bugger, is it twenty-past already? I'm supposed to be in Dales Court for a Standards Committee meeting. Never mind, I haven't had time to read the papers anyway. Do you think they'll miss me?

KIMBERLEY   They probably don't realize you're on it. You haven't been to a meeting since May.

HARRY   Look, I hate to ask you this, but can you do me a big favour and call Sue Graves to cancel my meeting about Learn Direct and this numeracy skills thing. I've got to prepare that communication class that Sarah asked me to do.

KIMBERLEY   But that's not till the end of next week, is it? You've cancelled on Sue twice already. I thought the basic skills project was your big career break?

HARRY   Look, I can't do everything. My desk is covered in crappy paperwork, I'm taking stuff home evenings and weekends, and I'm still letting people down. I've missed the kids' bedtimes twice this week.

KIMBERLEY   You do look awful.

HARRY	Thanks.
KIMBERLEY	So anyway, these messages . . .
HARRY	Forget it. I'm off. I've got to finish this marking before twelve, so I can go to something or other I've written on this post-it note and now can't bloody read. Now where did I put those assignments?
KIMBERLEY	Look, I'll email your messages to you.
HARRY	Don't bother, I never get time to read my emails . . .

Like all of us, Harry wonders sometimes why, when technological innovation, from dishwashers to computers, claims to save us time, we seem to have even less of it than ever. Partly, it is because technology can also overload us with more information than we know what to do with. But ironically it may also be our increasing obsession with 'managing' what we see as a scarce resource, which leads us as consumers to want everything more quickly. Society demands that more gets done in less time, because that is what we all want. Outside our Western corporate world, other cultures see time as plentiful. Frustrating though that may be to us in practice, this different perspective may be helpful occasionally.

'Time Management' is a comforting, but cruelly deceptive term. We do not really get to manage time, only manage ourselves within it. This is not about gimmicks or ready-made, near-leatherette diary systems, although they may help. It is about developing your own ways of remembering tasks, setting priorities, allocating time and avoiding wasteful activity. So, assuming we see time as in short supply, what can we do to make the most of it?

- Distinguish tasks from *purpose*. Ask yourself, what are you here for? What really is the point of your job? What do you want from your life, and how does work fit into this? Big questions, I know, but ones Harry clearly has not thought about, which is why time pressure forces him into continuous short-term thinking. Without an overall *purpose* decisions about priorities and objectives are built on sand.
- Agree *objectives*. If these are not forthcoming, then develop your own and give them to your manager, client, partner organization, or whatever. Make it clear this is what you will be working to, in the absence of any other input. Try to make these objectives SMART (see **O is for Objectives**).

- Distinguish *efficiency* from *effectiveness*. Efficiency is about doing the job right, effectiveness is about doing the right job. We inevitably have to make choices about what we do. The organized people focus their efforts on doing those things which fit best with their *purpose* and *objectives*, like Harry's meeting on numeracy skills, rather than spending time, as he no doubt will, making a fantastic job of an unimportant task.
- Separate *building* tasks from *maintenance* tasks. *Building* tasks help you to achieve your overall purpose and objectives. *Maintenance* tasks are the million things we have to respond to every day to keep things running. If we let these take over, we get that familiar sense of working our backside off getting nowhere. Plan in time for *building*. Otherwise, like Harry, you will be in constant reactive mode.
- Categorize activities by *urgency* and *importance*, and then plan your time. Try to allocate at least ten to fifteen minutes at the start of every day to this. How many students have you urged never to begin an exam question without planning? *Urgent* tasks must be done quickly, but may or may not be important. *Important* tasks are those which contribute to your purpose and objectives, and therefore deserve to have more time spent on them. We can see this as a matrix:

Category	Non-urgent	Urgent
Trivial	Why are you even doing this?	Do this straight away but be careful to allocate only a small amount of time to it (or delegate).
Important	Leave this till later but plan to spend a large chunk of time on it.	Allocate a large amount of time to this immediately.

Why not try analysing your current use of time by keeping a log for a few days. Then compare it to some of the points above. How are you doing? Can you consolidate more of your discretionary time, to give you space for the big important tasks?

In addition to these planning disciplines, getting more organized is about recognizing and avoiding the '*time wasters*'. By this we do not mean students and colleagues, but the following sort of things:

Telephone calls
- resist the temptation always to respond to a ringing phone. Make use of voicemail to give yourself quiet time, but ensure you regularly check messages.
- schedule time when you're available for calls and make this clear on voicemail messages.
- learn to say 'No'.
- avoid unstructured conversations. We've all encountered people who mistake talk for work.
- if you have the luxury of secretarial support, get calls filtered. If not, try caller recognition on your mobile!

Open door
- don't have chairs by your desk. Face the door to see callers.
- encourage people to make appointments.
- schedule 'drop-in' times.
- don't get caught in chat sessions. Tell people you are busy.

*Paperwork (see **P is for Paperwork**)*
- only handle it once. Make a decision.
- use bring forward files to get longer-term stuff out of the way.
- try categorizing it into *action, information, waste bin*.
- schedule time to clear it regularly.

Email
- like paperwork, take action the first time you look at it. Do not let it pile up. Respond immediately to any message you can.
- go through it once or twice daily (not every time you get a new message alert).
- make use of folders. Avoid printing emails out.
- when sending emails, indicate if you do not require an answer.
- take care who you give your address to. Use Spam filters.

Poor memory
- keep up-to-date 'to do' lists.
- use wall planners.
- keep a diary. Any sort you like, so long as there's only one! Block out time in it, and put in forward reminders.

Untidy desk
- don't hoard unfinished business. For some people mess is a constant and stressful symbol of how much they have to do.
- only have out the thing you are working on. File stuff away regularly.

Hopefully you will combine some or all of these tips into a self-organization routine which suits you. However, better work–life balance is also about a state of mind. We do not have to get seduced into a life view that treats everything as a job to be done as quickly as possible and ticked off our 'to do' list. What of reflection, learning and mental and spiritual renewal? Maybe some activities lend themselves better to a more abundant view of time and a less hectic approach to the business of living (see **Y is for You**). Try to work some of this into your life as well!

(NB You may also want to read **D is for Delegation** and **M is for Meetings**.)

H is for Charles Handy

Drawing on his experiences as a manager in the oil industry, an economist, a consultant and a professor at the London Business School, Charles Handy has become a leading British writer on the subject of organizations and management.

Much of his writing looks at the way organizations are structured and run, how social change is affecting this, and how all these changes impact upon employment relationships and the way we manage people. Handy takes leading concepts from management theorists on both sides of the Atlantic and makes them accessible to a wide audience by relating them to situations we all recognize. He uses the metaphor of differing tribes to describe the various cultures that can exist within an organization, and the metaphor of ancient Greek gods to explain the leadership styles which accompany these.

For Handy, the changing nature of work and people's expectations continue to raise questions about why we go to work and what truly motivates us. A demand for greater autonomy in decision-making and a growing emphasis on personal development have changed the character of the 'psychological contract' we have with our employer. More people seek some form of personal fulfilment from their work, and people are arguably more able and more inclined to go elsewhere if their organization does not provide it. As a result, jobs become less well-defined and constrained, and people have more licence to exercise their own judgement, outside a smaller core set of job requirements. He calls this the 'inside-out doughnut'.

All these continuing changes in the way society and organizations interact have important implications for how we manage people. Handy's work frequently alludes to examples from education, so it is perhaps no surprise that some of his thoughts on motivation will be familiar to any FE teacher:

- In order to motivate people by allowing them more discretion in how they do their jobs, we may paradoxically have to be more careful about how we specify the 'non-negotiable' outcomes the role must deliver.
- Rules and procedures tend to encourage a 'do nothing wrong' definition of success. If modern managers are to encourage continuous improvement and a degree of creativity, there must be a commitment to shared goals, and sufficient trust for people to try new things, make mistakes and learn.
- High performance is better served by building people's 'self-concept', by providing positive reinforcement of both good results and good behaviours.
- Given the importance of this 'self-concept' in motivation, the way managers organize work roles should avoid conflict and incompatibility between a person's role and their 'self-concept', that is their own view of their abilities, social position, ambition and personal values.
- Expectations can create self-fulfilling prophecies, and if we treat people as if they are poor performers, they will usually oblige us by acting that way (as educational research has shown). Managers with high expectations from their staff usually have better-motivated teams.

Handy outlines four 'dilemmas' for managers:

- *Cultures*: Since organizations are made up of several cultures, which may in turn adjust themselves to circumstance, how can the manager be flexible enough in their style and approach to be influential across all of these?
- *Timescales*: How can managers reconcile maintaining a focus on future direction with the challenge of responding successfully to short-term crises?
- *Trust & Control*: How does the manager keep his own boss happy with the team's results and quality while allowing individuals sufficient freedom to make mistakes and learn from them?
- *Commando Leader*: Many people's first taste of management is a discrete project with well-defined objectives and an enthusiastic team of experts to carry it through. Sadly, not all management is like this, so how do we learn to

cope with ambiguity, competing alternatives and multiple stakeholders?

Finally, we find Handy's analogy of the GP both instructive and uncomfortable. Like GPs, managers often have to identify the symptoms of a situation, diagnose the cause(s) and then determine the appropriate treatment and start applying it. Sadly, we often try to treat the symptoms, without getting to the bottom of their cause, or we issue the same prescription, regardless of symptoms ('What we need is better communications/a reorganization/a quality initiative/a training course').

If you'd like to read more of Charles Handy's ideas you'll find his work listed in the References at the end of the book.

H is for Heroines and Heroes of FE

The FE sector has its own heroines and heroes; women and men who have worked successfully to raise the profile of the sector and to fight FE's corner when it comes to status, funding, quality of provision and issues of inclusiveness and social justice. There isn't room here to include them all; but here are just a few of the stars who are currently (as we go to press) working hard on our behalf:

- Lynne Sedgmore CBE, Chief Executive of the Centre for Excellence in Leadership (CEL), providing professional development for the FE leaders of the future and working to address the lack of diversity among current leaders (see **E is for Equal opportunities**) and the immanent **Succession Crisis**.
- Alan Tuckett, Director of the National Institute for Adult Continuing Education (NIACE), currently working to motivate more adults to engage with learning and to extend access for low-waged workers.
- Ruth Silver CBE, Principal of Lewisham College, London, and advisor to the House of Commons select committee, contributing to national education policy.
- Dr John Brennan, Chief Executive of the Association of Colleges (AoC), whose advocacy for FE has included: challenging Ofsted's criticism of FE colleges as 'inappropriate' (2004); arguing that FE is equally important to the success of 'UK plc as Higher Education (HE), (2005); and presenting the case for colleges as 'the engine for the skills revolution' (2006).

You will no doubt have FE heroes and heroines of your own to add to this list.

H is for Human Resources

Human resources are people. You yourself are a human resource and, hopefully, by browsing this *A–Z*, you are in the process of making yourself an even more valuable and effective one. It is often argued that in FE every manager is a Human Resource Manager because every manager is, in one way or another, managing people. Whatever your specific managerial role at the moment, you will need to know something about:

- the role of the HR Manager in FE; and
- the HR responsibilities of an FE line manager (someone in a post like yours, perhaps).

In the days before incorporation in 1993, few FE college organizational structures included posts for Human Resource or Personnel Managers because Local Authorities (at that time known as Local Education Authorities: LEAs) were responsible for the human resourcing and personnel functions. However, since colleges have grown into their role as corporate bodies and have taken responsibility for the recruitment and management of their staff, the HR function has become a central and key part of college management structures.

The functions of the HR Manager include:

- staff recruitment, selection and contractual arrangements
- maintaining a balance between organizational and individual performance. This will include such things as appraisals, staff training and development.
- staff relations and industrial relations (for example, issues involving Trade Unions), Health and Safety issues, and **disciplinary** procedures

One of the requirements of an HR Manager in FE is a working

knowledge of employment law and the college policies that interpret it. Since incorporation, colleges have needed to develop a wide range of HR policies in order to undertake their HR responsibilities under the terms of their articles of incorporation, and in order to comply with employment law nationally. Typically these policies will cover such areas as **recruitment**, redundancy, **discipline** and **equal opportunities**. These policies and HR specialists, however, do not take away the responsibility of all line managers in FE (and this will include you) to manage their own teams effectively, fairly and in line with current legislation. It is the line manager's responsibility to a) follow exactly the procedures set down in college policy and b) to ensure that the colleagues they manage have access to all necessary guidelines and that they receive appropriate advice as necessary.

I is for Inspection

There is an Ofsted inspection coming up at Bogginbrook College and, while Sheena is using her one free hour of the week to sort out some pre-inspection documentation in the office, she overhears the following conversation between the VP and Parveen, her Head of School, as they stand talking in the foyer.

PARVEEN The trouble is, I'm having to do everything myself.

VP Surely you can get the people in your school to sort out some of the paperwork?

PARVEEN Well yes, you'd think so, wouldn't you? But the trouble is I just wouldn't be able to trust them to get it done. They're hopeless. I wouldn't be surprised if they set out to sabotage the whole thing.

VP Why on earth would they do that?

PARVEEN To get at me. After all, the inspection grade is going to reflect on me and how I run this School. It's not going to bother them, is it?

VP Well . . .

PARVEEN And I just hope Sheena doesn't set out to rock the boat. I wouldn't put it past her.

VP Oh dear. I didn't realize.

We all know that Parveen is wrong here on a number of counts. Inspections *aren't* there as an opportunity for managers to set out on an ego trip or to try to show that they run their section, school or department single-handed. Indeed, part of the purpose of inspections is to evaluate team effectiveness. And they *do* have an impact on the stress levels and self-esteem of individual teachers and teaching teams. And we know that Sheena is conscientiously pulling her weight. What's happening here is that Parveen is openly demonstrating a) that she is stressed beyond the point where she can act rationally or with discretion, and b) that she has – unjustly – no faith in her team to rise to the occasion or behave professionally. These are the two worst mistakes a manager can make when preparing for an inspection.

Before incorporation, FE colleges were subject to occasional inspections by HMI (Her Majesty's Inspectorate) and by their LEA (Local Education Authority) inspectors. Since incorporation, inspection has become almost a way of life, with inspections at first carried out by the FEFC (FE Funding Council) inspectorate, and then subsequently by Ofsted and ALI. One of the most productive – but also from an FE manager's point of view most time-consuming – practices to have arisen from the current inspection regime is the college Self-Assessment. The regular cycle of self-assessments will inevitably involve you, as a manager, in a number of additional activities including audits and observations. Here are three pieces of advice that will be helpful to you in preparing for a Self-Assessment exercise or a formal Ofsted inspection.

- Ofsted inspection reports on FE colleges are posted on the Ofsted website and make very useful reading. Certain themes emerge there. For example, inspections in several colleges may discover difficulties in the effective management of small teams, or poor communication within or between designated teams. From your point of view as a manager this is valuable intelligence. It alerts you to which areas of practice may come under particular scrutiny, and allows you to examine and revise policies and practices within your own team.
- Members of your team are certain to feel increased levels of stress when facing an inspection. Even if this is 'only' a Self-Assessment, it's likely to involve graded observations of their teaching. While you yourself may feel snowed under with paperwork, meetings and other administrative duties generated by assessments and inspections, you will still need to remember that every individual in your team is having their own reaction to process, and it's highly unlikely that anyone is entirely immune to the general sense of stress which inspections generate. So, however stretched you feel, this still calls for a sympathetic attitude on your part and a great deal of cheer-leading, morale-boosting and confidence-building. All three

of these are more easily accomplished if you have gained the trust of your team and demonstrated that you trust them in return. The worst possible line to take is the one Parveen takes with Sheena.

- Keep in mind that there is a clear distinction between observations of teaching carried out for developmental purposes, as in appraisals or on CPD programmes, for example, and those carried out for judgemental purposes, as in a self-assessment or inspection. Although both have the declared purpose of contributing towards an improvement in practice, from the point of view of the teacher being observed, judgmental feedback (*This is your grade. This categorizes your current level of skill as a teacher*) feels very different from developmental feedback (*This is what I saw. Do you feel there are ways you'd like to improve on this?*). Whether the observations are performed by yourself or by an inspector, it is your task, as manager, to *ensure that judgements made are discussed and acted on in such a way as to raise quality of provision rather than lower teacher morale* (see **F is for Feedback**)

For latest Ofsted reports on FE colleges go to: www.ofsted.gov.uk (accessed 17/05/06).

I is for Interviews

Among the most crucial skills for a manager in FE is that of having productive one-to-one conversations with other people. These may be members of your team, colleagues, prospective employees, outside agencies or students. The context may be recruitment, coaching, appraisal, discipline, negotiation or joint problem-solving. But there are certain core skills which you can learn once and apply in all of these situations. These are: Managing the Environment, Building Rapport, Recognizing Non-Verbal Cues, Asking Good Questions, Active Listening and Closing.

Managing the environment

This is all about creating the appropriate conditions for a successful conversation. Generally this means:

- conduct your interviews in a place which is comfortable but businesslike (i.e. not on hard chairs in a bare, windowless office, but equally not sitting on the bed in a hotel room!).
- find a place where you will not be overheard or interrupted. Respect people's need for confidentiality. Telephone calls should be diverted, and ideally the door closed or even a 'Please do not disturb' sign clearly displayed on the door. Mobile phones and pagers should be switched off.
- try to arrange the furniture in such a way as to make you both feel at ease and free to talk. Interviews conducted across desks are to be avoided, as are different types or levels of seating.
- be on time. It is discourteous to people to do otherwise.

Building rapport

Productive conversations usually depend upon an open and honest exchange of information, and you are more likely to get this if you

devote some effort to helping the other person relax. Even negotiation and disciplinary encounters are best addressed as opportunities
for mutual problem-solving, and this usually means finding common
ground.

- avoid leaping straight in with tough questions or challenges.
  Give the other person an opportunity to relax and settle into
  the interview. Indulge in small talk. Find something they are
  comfortable talking about.
- it is useful to begin with an explanation of the nature and
  structure of the interview, what you want to discuss, and an
  idea of how long it is intended to last.
- try to match your body language with theirs, but maintain
  an open posture, avoiding defensive gestures such as crossed
  arms.
- maintain regular eye contact.
- if taking notes during the interview, inform the interviewee
  in advance.
- invite questions.

Recognizing non-verbal cues
There are those who have made a detailed study of this topic, and
claim to read all sorts of covert messages into our every look and
gesture. But for us lay people, the important thing to remember is
that less than 10 per cent of communication may be conveyed by
the actual words we say (Mehrabian 1972). The other thing to
remember is that common sense can go a long way.

- Conversation means taking turns. Learning to recognize what
  people do when they feel it's their turn can help us manage
  how much we say. This includes leaning forward, clearing
  their throat, raising their head and opening their lips, among
  other things. We all know people who are resolutely blind to
  all these cues, and you do not want to get next to them at a
  party.
- Watch out for changes of facial expression. Frowning, for
  example, may indicate lack of understanding or disagreement.
  It may be time for a question. Taut facial muscles and pursed
  lips may indicate you are on the wrong tack!
- Similarly we may able to detect how engaged someone is

with what we are saying by whether they lean forward and look animated or dissociate themselves by leaning back and looking away.

Asking good questions

Let us remind ourselves of some of the different sorts of questions and how we might use them.

Open questions
Questions that require more than a simple yes or no answer:

- Tell me about . . .
- What would you like to discuss?
- How did you feel about . . .?

These are the questions that are great for exploring issues and getting information, so good interviewers tend to use them most.

Probe questions
Questions that follow up a topic in more detail.

- What do you mean when you say . . .?
- Tell me a bit more about . . .?
- How do you know . . .?

Good for finding out more detail or challenging glib statements, these are used to ensure that issues have been fully examined, and assumptions not taken for granted.

Hypothetical questions
These questions open the mind to new possibilities.

- What if you were to . . .?
- What would be the consequences if . . .?
- How would you feel about . . .?

Useful for testing people's position on an issue, or their commitment to a course of action, but beware, these questions can allow job applicants to impress with what they *might* have done, instead of what they *did* do. They can also turn into leading questions (see page 69).

Link questions
Questions which seek to understand the connection between ideas and events.

- So, if you say you cannot do . . . what will that mean for . . .?
- How will you . . . if . . .?
- You say you do this, and that this often happens . . . Are these two things connected?

These are good for prompting new understanding and helping someone explore cause and effect.

Closed questions
Questions that generally have a yes or no answer. Excessive use of these can turn a conversation into a session of twenty questions, particularly with someone who is shy or inclined to be monosyllabic. Used in moderation, however, for clarification or probing, they can help to avoid misunderstandings.

- So this happened last week?
- Are you saying you have tried this?
- Will you have this done by . . .?

Leading questions
Questions which invite a particular answer by the way they are phrased.

- So, do you think your problem is . . .?
- I expect you were just feeling a bit off, were you?
- I guess at that point you . . . did you?

These are to be avoided, generally, as they disguise the facts and smack of manipulation.

Active listening
In any one-to-one interchange, it is not enough just to listen. We have to show we are listening. This is often referred to as 'active listening'.

Active listening is the skill of concentrating on what someone is saying and demonstrating that you have heard and understood what they have said. Here is a reminder of some of the ways we can listen actively:

- Do not start thinking of your next question as soon as you've asked the previous one.
- If you must write notes, try to keep them brief, or stop the conversation to write them.
- Do not be afraid of silence.
- Do not interrupt, but if things are getting off the point, steer the discussion back at the first available opportunity, perhaps by saying, 'I'm sorry, may I ask about something else?'
- Watch your body language. Remember, leaning forward and nodding demonstrates interest. Leaning back, folding your arms and looking at the ceiling does not.
- Make encouraging noises (Uh-huh . . . right . . . yes . . . I see . . . tell me more . . . really?)
- Summarize to help check understanding.
- In most cases you should aim for the other person to talk for at least 70 per cent of the time.

Closing
Any productive conversation should have an outcome. Do not finish one without articulating what this is.

- Summarize what has been discussed. Check for mutual understanding.
- Ensure you both leave with an agreed outcome, ideally some action, even if this is that you need to meet again.
- Say what will happen next, along with any communication processes and what timescales can be expected.

J is for JFDI

An acronym that will already be familiar to many, JFDI stands for *Just Flipping Do It*, or words to that effect. Its relevance here is threefold.

First, as a general rule, all good managers learn to recognize when the discussion and mulling over and planning must give way to the process of actually doing something. Sheena has suggested to Parveen that some changes to the delivery of the Care Management NVQ programme may enable more convenient timetabling. As a result, she's got the job of doing it.

- she has agreed clear objectives as to what will be delivered (see **O is for Objectives**).
- perhaps she has assembled a competent project team composed of relevant people.
- she may have identified local 'champions' around the college who will help.
- she has agreed who is accountable for what and clarified the limits of her own authority.
- she has (hopefully) devised success criteria that will ultimately tell her whether she has achieved what she planned to.
- she has maybe analysed who the stakeholders are in this issue, and who will support, who will put up resistance and who will be neutral.
- she has clearly communicated what she wants to do, and tried to manage people's expectations.
- she has set out a process for monitoring progress towards the objectives.

In other words, she has dutifully followed many of the rules of good project management.

But she will not have all the information she would like and, because life is occasionally unpredictable, she will never have accounted for everything. We must therefore recognize the point at which the only way to learn more is to take action and see what happens. As soon as we start to implement anything we change things (see **C is for Change**), and because things in organizations are interconnected, this may change the entire 'playing field' on which we are operating, affect people's responses and support (or lack of it) and therefore affect the way we wish to proceed with our project. Retaining this flexibility means knowing when to stop initial planning, try something, see what happens and learn from it for the rest of the plan. This is why many successful projects start with a pilot or trial, because often the only way to see what works is to try it. 'A bad decision is better than no decision' has become a management cliché, but it captures a significant truth. The idea that lots of small, related change activities can reach a point where much wider systemic change in an organization is accelerated stems from recent concepts such as chaos theory and 'tipping points'. These have been applied to various phenomena, including climate change.

Secondly, these thoughts may also be relevant to those faced with yet another 'strategic initiative', launched from on high, outside the college itself.

It is always tempting in such circumstances, to do your King Lear impression, railing against the elements to whichever poor colleague happens to have wandered by. If you feel that there is about as much chance of government listening to you as there was the storm listening to Lear, then here's an alternative strategy. Express your professional opinion, by all means, then move through the kind of planning disciplines mentioned above (sometimes this very process can expose fatal flaws in the project), but then, importantly, take some action and get a result. At least you will feel in control, and if no one else chooses to learn from the outcomes, at least you will.

Which brings us to our third application of JFDI: your own self-development. We all know people's learning styles vary, and some have a greater preference for experimentation than others. But, whatever learning style we find most comfortable, the learning cycle (Kolb 1983) cannot function without us taking action. A desire to make the perfect plan, or an understandable fear of failure can hold us back, but we know from experience with our students that having a go, learning from it and trying a different tack is more conducive to development and personal growth. The same goes for managers, which is why our reaction to our team's mistakes can have such an impact on the culture we create.

K is for Kanter

Rosabeth Kanter's (1983) book, *Changemasters*, is worth a read if you are at all interested in what makes innovations succeed or fail; and as a manager in FE you certainly should be.

Here's an innovation that didn't even make it to the starting line:

SHEENA   Parveen, I know you're busy, but can I have a quick word?

PARVEEN   You're quite right. I am busy. What is it?

SHEENA   I've had this idea . . .

PARVEEN   (Sighs) Not another one . . .

SHEENA   I've thought of a way we could make really good use of the VLP . . . You know, the Virtual Learning Portal.

PARVEEN   Too expensive. Can't get students to use it, anyway. Is that all?

SHEENA   But I think I've found a way we could save on costs and . . .

PARVEEN   Anything to do with finance you'll have to clear with the VP and the Finance Office. Sorry. That's my phone. I have to go.

In the Lifelong Learning sector, we hear a great deal about innovation, which is not surprising, given the rate of change we experience. Kanter provides an interesting list of reasons why an innovation may fail. In doing so, she is helping us to look at ways in which management can be responsible for the success or failure not only of a specific innovation but also of the innovative spirit – the will to innovate – which may originate from the individuals or teams we manage. She gives the list the ironic title: *Rules for Stifling Innovation* (Kanter 1983: 100). Those that might apply in an FE context can be paraphrased like this:

- respond suspiciously to new ideas from those you manage.
- make sure no one acts on a new idea without securing permission from several tiers of management.
- be free with your criticism and stingy with your praise.
- if anyone identifies a problem, interpret it as failure.
- keep rigid control of everything.
- spring decisions on your team without warning or consultation.
- don't share or release information without a struggle.

Parveen managed to cover several of these during her very short exchange with Sheena. And we've seen managers indulging in some of these behaviours elsewhere in this *A–Z* (for example, in **B is for Bullying**). But let's have a look at what might happen if a manager has read Kanter, made a mental note not to fall into any of the errors on that list, and one day is stopped in the corridor by Raj who says:

Sarah! Have you got a minute? I just want to run an idea past you . . .

SARAH	Yep. Go ahead. Mind if we keep walking?
RAJ	That's fine, yeah. I just wanted to suggest a different way we might do the teaching for the Advanced group. They really need tutorial support, a lot of them; and we don't have the timetable time. But if we could use the VLP to give them some of the input . . .
SARAH	We'd free up the time for tutorials. Good thinking.
RAJ	I could work it all out – the hours and everything – but I'd need the timetabling information and I'm not sure how we cost the work of putting stuff up on the VLP, but . . .
SARAH	No problem. You can get all that from Norman. Tell him I said so. And if you hit any snags let me know. When you've written it up, costings and stuff, we'll have a look at where we go from there. The rest of the team OK with this?
RAJ	Dead keen.
SARAH	Great. Oh, and Raj?
RAJ	Yeah?
SARAH	Well done.

And well done, Sarah. This is the way to encourage what we might call 'bottom–up' innovation. Raj is having his initiative and enthusiasm rewarded by encouragement and praise, which makes it all the more likely that he'll continue to come up with good ideas and will maintain a high level of motivation. In other words, Sarah is ensuring that he remains an asset to the team.

But what about when the innovation originates with management? Or even from outside the college altogether, as some curriculum initiatives do? The issue for management then is no longer about stifling or encouragement, but about carrying staff along in the direction management has chosen, or been required, to go. For a full discussion of this issue, see **C is for Change**.

L is for Leadership

At several points in this *A–Z* we have used the terms 'management' and 'leadership', so we thought it might be helpful to say something about how these terms might be interpreted.

Many commentators, among them Warren Bennis, to whom we have devoted a separate section, and John Kotter, another American academic, have drawn a clear distinction between management and leadership. These comparisons generally portray management as a somewhat static, rule-bound and transactional process for ensuring that things get done efficiently. Leadership, on the other hand, is an altogether more sexy approach, which involves creating a compelling vision of the future, inspiring followers, developing people and promoting continuous change.

More specifically, in his book, *On Becoming a Leader* (1989), Bennis associates management with administration, systems, structure, control and maintaining the status quo. In contrast, leadership he sees as being about innovation, development, people, inspiring trust, taking the long view and challenging the accepted way of doing things. Certainly there is a compelling logic about these distinctions, and we can all think of individuals who epitomize one model rather than the other. It is also fair to say that leadership is a useful concept in modern organizations which may increasingly look to emphasize the ability of employees at all levels to display this quality. Many of its features can be viewed as independent of status or title. The same is not so true of management. This concept that leadership can be found and developed at all levels is sometimes referred to as 'distributed leadership', and used as another category, alongside transactional and **transformational** leadership in, for example, the 2005 Learning and Skills Research Centre report, *Leadership, development and diversity in the learning and skills sector.*

However, ultimately, we see these sorts of distinctions as potentially unhelpful to managers in colleges, at all levels, trying to do their best to meet conflicting demands from a variety of stakeholders. Making a kind of 'second-class citizen' out of the necessary work of sound execution and delivery undervalues the work of diligent managers toiling away at making things happen, sometimes against the odds. Rather than making management and leadership appear mutually exclusive, it might be more helpful to see these definitions, as Kotter does, as complementary parts of a single role, at whatever level it is practised. After all, there are surely not many organizations that have jobs for 'managers' who cannot inspire, motivate and develop their teams, or for 'leaders' who can communicate a compelling vision of the future, but cannot ensure the steps are put in place to get there.

M is for Managing Upwards

Harry and Angela, Section Leaders at Bogginbrook College of Further Education, have been having a bad week/month/year and are venting their spleen over a coffee in the 'Mega-Bites' snack bar.

HARRY   Sorry, I can't be long. I seem to have just acquired another job. That's four now, I think, or is it five? Any idea what 'Benchmarking training standards' might involve?

ANGELA   No, but I'll bet it doesn't involve doing the job you're actually paid for. Remember when you had time to do that properly?

HARRY   I dunno, it's kind of flattering to be asked to do these things. It's just that I feel so dumped on. The senior team are under pressure about achievement rates and the private sector mob muscling in on skills training, so muggins here gets handed another exercise in self-justification, rather than having the chance to actually improve things.

ANGELA   Ah well, ours is not to question why, ours is but to lump it or go get a decently paid job.

HARRY   They just don't know what they want. They adopt this knee-jerk response to every report or initiative that comes out of government without any sense of a long-term strategy or objectives. So I'm just going to end up buggering around from pillar to post, trying to get my hands on information that shows what a great job we're doing from people who won't give it to me because they're scared it might show the exact opposite!

ANGELA   You should just tell them where to shove their 'Benchmarking', and stick to what's on your job description.

HARRY   Well, I've got to admit, I did let Parveen have it a bit this
            time. Told her why it was so difficult. I've got no time.
            I'm snowed under with paperwork as it is. The people
            I need to talk to won't cooperate. The objectives aren't
            clear enough. And employers won't give a toss about the
            results anyway.

ANGELA   There you go! So why bother?

HARRY   Because I'll still get bollocked from here to kingdom
            come, if it's not done how they want . . .

If any of this sounds vaguely familiar, you are not alone. Not only
in Further Education, but in all sorts of organizations throughout
the world, managers experience the frustrations of feeling trapped
between the competing demands of their customers/clients/
learners and their teams and the senior managers they report to.
If the sector or organization is going through a lot of change (and
what organization isn't?) then the conflict and stress will be all the
more acute.

This is often presented as exclusively a middle-management
dilemma, but the truth is that managers and team leaders at all levels
in a college have a 'boss' somewhere, whose priorities may not
always appear consistent with their own or their team's. As a consequence, canteens, water-coolers and corridors everywhere ring
to cries of 'What the hell do they think they're doing?' and 'I don't
know what they want any more!' and 'Why don't they ever listen
to me?', as virtually everyone in the organization blames the mythical
'they' for all their anxieties and frustrations.

But, consider for a moment that our little vignette is also an
illustration of how disempowering self-talk can keep us in the role
of victim and convince us all that there is nothing to be done.
Instead of focusing on the things we may like to complain about,
what if we were to look at what it *is* in our power to change? Can
we change our own behaviour to 'manage' relationships with our
own bosses (and peer group) more effectively?

A helpful way into this is simply to think about what you value in
those who report to you. Here are some thoughts:

- *Take a coaching/mentoring approach*: particularly if you feel at
  odds with what is being proposed, try asking questions,
  listening and summarizing to explore possible areas of

compromise, or to improve mutual understanding. (Of course, if digging your trench, getting in and putting your tin hat on has ever actually worked for you, then by all means stick with that . . .). Master the art of disagreeing without being disagreeable.

- *Agree SMART objectives*: help your boss by suggesting ways of making objectives for a task/project more specific, measurable, realistic and time-bound (see **O is for Objectives**).
- *Take responsibility*: if things appear muddled, suggest an agenda. Be clear about what can be done, but be helpful, not obstructive.
- *Agree and forget*: what every boss wants. Once everything is clear and agreed, it will get done on time or you will go back and keep her posted. No one likes to be chased so don't give her a reason to do this.
- *No surprises*: none of us likes to be caught out, particularly in front of *our* boss. So get into the habit of regular informal communication with your manager to keep them informed of progress.
- *Talk solutions not problems*: instead of thinking of a hundred reasons why something cannot be done, try to go armed with alternatives.
- *Ask for help*: don't be afraid to admit what you don't know, but accompany this with a willingness to learn. We are all secretly flattered by requests to use our expertise and knowledge to help a colleague.
- *Ask for and respond positively to feedback*: your boss might not, so help him by modelling the behaviour of someone who believes in lifelong learning!
- *Build, maintain and use your networks*: you may actually have influence that your boss lacks in some quarters. You may have been around longer, or just forged stronger relationships with certain people. Can you help smooth the way?
- *Adapt your influencing style*: find what works best with different people, but remember that gaining and keeping rapport, asking questions, listening actively, summarizing benefits, and working towards a decision, will always help.

This is not about being an inveterate boot-licker or senior management 'clone'. On the contrary, it is about taking control and choosing to act and be treated as a responsible adult who believes they can and should influence what is going on.

M is for Market

We are accustomed now to thinking of ourselves in FE as competitors in a market for post-compulsory education and training. This wasn't always the case. The Further and Higher Education Act (1992) marked a changing point in the provision of post-compulsory education. It was an enactment of the proposals set out in the 1991 **White Paper**, *Education and Training for the 21st Century*, one of the most far-reaching of which was that FE Colleges, (and also sixth-form and tertiary colleges) were to be removed from the control of Local Authorities, then known as Local Education Authorities (LEAs). This transformation of FE Colleges into corporate bodies became known as *incorporation* and marked the real beginning of a 'quasi-market' in FE, as colleges whose provision had previously been managed and agreed strategically under regulation by the LEAs began to operate as individual corporate organizations. Competition for students now sometimes began to involve offering courses and qualifications which duplicated provision in neighbouring colleges and sixth forms. The necessity to compete in a crowded market has created the current situation in which stronger (larger, better resourced, or more entrepreneurial) colleges thrive at the expense of others which have competed less successfully in the market. This has inevitably led to some college closures and **mergers (**see **M is for Mergers)**. In addition, by encouraging schools to include vocational education in their post–16 curriculum with the introduction of general national vocational qualifications (GNVQs), the 1992 Act was also responsible for creating further competition between schools and colleges for attracting or retaining pupils at 16. In a number of ways, therefore, the Further and Higher Education Act of 1992 was responsible for pushing the tertiary sector of education firmly into the world of competition and market forces.

This has brought about fundamental changes to the nature of the manager's role in FE. The imperatives of the market, with its emphasis on competition and survival, are shifting the focus of management away from purely curriculum issues and increasingly towards concerns about funding, cost-effectiveness and statistical returns. This may make the role of FE manager more challenging and fulfilling, but it can have another consequence too, which is a widening gap between the agendas of the managers and those whom they manage. For colleagues in FE who are primarily teachers, the important agenda is naturally about pedagogic and curriculum issues; while the agenda of many managers is domin-ated – whether they like it or not – by financial and strategic demands. This apparent lack of a common agenda can lead to mis-communications and misunderstandings which require careful management to resolve. And for those managers who also retain a substantial teaching role – such as subject and team leaders – these competing agendas can be the cause of role conflict and stress if left unacknowledged and unaddressed.

However, we're looking here at competing agendas, but not necessarily at conflicting ones. Curriculum, pedagogy, targets and funding are all issues to be addressed in the interests of raising and sustaining a good quality of provision for the FE learner.

M is for Meetings

Norman has convened a meeting.

O.K. is everyone here? . . . Angela's late as usual. I wonder if I told her it had changed from Room 6? . . . Well, let's just start without her. She hasn't made the last three meetings anyway. OK folks. Sorry I didn't get the agenda out before, but I've got some copies here, if you'll just pass them round . . . You might have to share . . .

I don't think there're any matters arising. We didn't really come to any firm conclusions last time, I seem to remember, so perhaps we should just go round the table and see where we're each at on this one . . . er, Harry . . . Harry! . . . Could we just have one meeting please . . .?

Sound familiar? We probably all spend more time than we would like in apparently pointless and sometimes badly run meetings which seem to go on for ever and achieve very little. So why not just ban them altogether (or avoid them, like Angela)?

Tempting, I know; but the truth is that meetings do serve a very important purpose, several in fact:

- they help to define the team and establish collective identity.
- they combine the knowledge, experience and creativity of the group to produce more powerful and cohesive decisions.
- they create commitment and mobilize people into action.
- they share information and improve communication.

Well, that's the theory, at least. What may actually happen is this:

- As a result of galloping megalomania, or insecurity, or both, the chairperson just uses the group to rubber-stamp plans he/she has already decided upon.
- The proceedings are entirely dominated by a few individuals who talk endlessly and say very little. (When they're not in

meetings, they sit next to you on the train and talk on their mobile phone.)
- You all have an amusing/riveting/stultifying discussion for three hours, sometimes – if you're really lucky – followed by a rather pleasant lunch, and two days later no one can remember what was said.

Of course, we never run meetings like this, do we? No, because we follow a few simple guidelines:

A meeting? Are you sure?
- Don't have a meeting just because it's Thursday or the month end or your predecessor used to have one. Some meetings may be mandatory, but assuming you are calling the meeting, only have it if it will fulfil one of the purposes above, and even then, only if there is not a more effective way of achieving the same end.

Get yourself organized
- If it is your meeting, prepare an agenda, or some definite objectives for the meeting and circulate 2–3 days before. If it is not your meeting – for example, if representatives of the LSC or the DfES have requested a meeting at the college – it is reasonable to ask for and expect that they will provide you in good time with an agenda. (Tip: if no one can come up with objectives or an agenda, you could suggest that you don't need a meeting.)
- If you are putting the agenda together, order it logically (e.g. lively, creative activity early on).
- Try to keep topics covered to what can be achieved in two hours max.
- Be alert and sensitive to matters which may divide the group.
- Wherever possible, give people in advance any lengthy stuff that needs to be read, at the same time as you give them details of time, venue, etc. And then maybe even remind them when the meeting's about to come up, so that they remember to do the reading as well as attend.
- Sort out the seating arrangements, audio-visual kit, etc. in advance of the meeting.

Make the discussion count
What you're usually aiming to do as chair is:

- define the issue/problem
- collect all available and relevant facts/opinions
- generate alternatives before agreeing a diagnosis or solution
- decide on a course of action

Be a 'servant' to the group and don't take sides
- Listen (we often devalue this in meetings, accusing people of not making much of a contribution when they may simply be reflecting on matters).
- Ensure all are motivated and involved, including the quiet ones, even if this means politely shutting others up.
- Summarize all the way through, and check understanding.
- Keep group focused on objectives.
- Make sure there is consensus and conclusions are reached, or further actions agreed. (If you have a lot of meetings without this happening, you may want to question what purpose they are serving!)

Nail it down
- Finally summarize discussion and review against the objectives of the meeting.
- Leave people feeling something has been achieved.
- Remind people of actions, when they are required and from whom.
- Never action someone not at the meeting (though this is always tempting!).
- Never let the discussion ramble on once agreement is reached.
- As a minimum, make sure a note is kept of time/date/ location, who attended, a list of what was discussed and actions agreed by name/date. When you come to put documentation together for the next Ofsted or QAA visit you'll be pleased to have nice, orderly records of all meetings held.

M is for Mentoring and Coaching

These terms are often used to describe two different processes. But in education, mentoring is probably the more familiar term, and it has become an accepted way of describing a wide range of one-to-one support. We will sidestep the semantic debate here by using the term 'mentoring' to include also the kind of performance-improvement discussions more commonly described as coaching.

These days there's more emphasis on mentoring in FE than ever before. This is partly due to the higher profile being given to specialist subject support in teaching standards for the lifelong learning sector. As a result, the quality of mentoring within colleges is coming under increasing scrutiny during inspections and self-assessment exercises. Although in an FE context we are accustomed to think of mentoring largely in relation to the support of newly qualified or newly appointed teachers, managers can benefit from mentoring, too, as you may already have discovered for yourself.

So let's have a look at a recent meeting between mentor and mentee at Bogginbrook College. Parveen is Harry's mentor.

PARVEEN   Hi Harry, come in. How are you feeling today?
HARRY   Er . . . fine thanks.
PARVEEN   That's fantastic Harry. I'm so pleased we could have this time together. I thought it would be an opportunity for us to dialogue, and explore how you're settling into the new job.
HARRY   Oh, great, really good. I'm enjoying it so far. Well, it's all a bit unfamiliar, you know, but no . . . I'm good . . .
PARVEEN   Great, cool. Let's unpick that a bit, shall we Harry?
HARRY   How do you mean?

PARVEEN   Well, it sounds as though something's troubling you, something you perhaps feel it's hard to talk about.

HARRY   No, not really. I just need to find my feet that's all. Get to know my way around. I suppose I'm still learning who everyone is.

PARVEEN   I understand. And how does that make you feel, Harry? A bit of a stranger? An outsider? Like you're lost?

HARRY   No, I hadn't really thought any of those things . . . until now.

PARVEEN   Good, because I want you to know how much we value you as a person, as well as a colleague. I want you to know, Harry, that you can be anything you want to be.

HARRY   Well, I just want to be a reasonably competent section leader at the minute.

PARVEEN   Great! So now we're starting to build goals. Say with me 'I can overcome anything to reach my goals'. Come on, let's hold hands while we say it, and try to picture what you'll look like when you're a reasonably competent section leader.

HARRY   Is this some sort of initiation ceremony?

PARVEEN   Gosh, Harry, that's an interesting comment. Why do you think you felt the need to say that? . . .

Oh dear. Mentoring, as a management and leadership approach, is becoming more and more mainstream, as people realize how effective it can be. But there is still some confusion about what exactly mentoring is, and a degree of suspicion about why one would want it. It can all seem a bit 'new age' and 'touchy-feely'. Parveen, with her patronizing self-help manual mind games, and evangelical desire to uncover some hidden psychosis that she can 'cure', is doing nothing to dispel this suspicion.

Mentoring is not psychotherapy, nor is it having an expert solve all your problems for you. It is usually a series of conversations, which help a person to learn, change or come to decisions in a way that enables them to achieve their objectives or get better at what they do. The principle, as with much adult learning, is that people are more motivated to learn when they are helped to find their own answers, and encouraged to reflect on their experiences, good and bad, in order to gain insights which help them to improve.

When mentoring, a manager will use skills such as questioning, listening, summarizing and feedback to help the person make sense of their circumstances and experience (see **A is for Appraisal, F is for Feedback, I is for Interviews**). It often starts from an appreciation of the individual's strengths, on the grounds that this can motivate people and boost their confidence. It can also help them to see how they might better use their strengths to overcome any development needs.

If this all sounds a bit 'soft', don't be fooled. Imagine this: you are asked to examine your own performance and take on board feedback, then you are challenged to make sense of this for your own learning, to agree specific and measurable (SMART) goals and to commit to an action plan to help you achieve them (see **O is for Objectives**). This is actually a pretty tough regime. But that's what being effectively mentored is about. Just being told what to do or how to get it right is an awful lot easier. Unfortunately, of course, we do not learn very much that way.

So, aside from it being about learning and performance improvement and consisting of a lot of questioning, listening, feedback and goal-setting, what else is it that characterizes effective mentoring? Principally two things:

- the nature of the relationship
- the structure of the conversations

The nature of the relationship

A mentoring *relationship* is based on:

Trust and support
In order to talk honestly about your experiences, feelings and development needs, you have to be sure that the person sitting opposite is prepared to suspend judgement, has your best interests at heart, and believes you are capable of learning and developing further. This is why mixing the role of immediate line manager and mentor can be tricky!

Rapport
Without this you are unlikely to be open about yourself or take on board feedback, however constructive.

A shared agenda
Aims, objectives and feedback are ineffective if they are imposed. If the person being mentored (the 'mentee') doesn't set the agenda themselves, they must at least take part in developing and agreeing it, together with their mentor.

Discovery
Mentoring works by helping someone arrive at their own learning through skilful questioning and listening, not by instruction or direction. Feedback should be offered impartially, and where information or suggestions are appropriate, the mentor should earn permission to offer them. In an effective and supportive mentoring relationship mistakes can be embraced as an opportunity to learn.

Joint problem-solving
Like discovery, this challenges the 'I know best, so do as I say' approach to management, and encourages a style based on pooling information, ideas and learning in a more collaborative way. Questioning and challenge are seen as a prelude to learning and improvement, and not as the mentee trying to show you up and take over your job.

The structure of the conversations
So, how do we *structure* a mentoring conversation? There are many helpful models, especially in the coaching literature, and you can discover some for yourself in the books we refer to in the list of useful references. But here are some things these models tend to have in common:

Contracting
Early on in a mentoring relationship the parties need to agree a few ground rules concerning meetings, confidentiality, what mentoring is, how it fits with other processes and relationships, and who is responsible for what. This helps prevent all sorts of later difficulties, such as your mentee chasing you down the corridor on a very busy day begging for an immediate meeting.

Identifying opportunities

The next step is to explore what the mentoring can help with. This involves reviewing a person's experiences, identifying strengths, understanding where they may have struggled and helping them to formulate an action plan incorporating the necessary national or institutional standards, or, where appropriate, to devise their own clear and measurable objectives for learning, change and improvement.

Experimentation & reflection

The mentee may then want to think through or try out different options, new techniques or ideas, and reflect on how effective these are in helping them achieve their objectives.

Commitment to action

All this effort is wasted unless it results in some action by the mentee, which of course leads to more learning. So the aim of any mentoring conversation, and every series of conversations, is to agree SMART objectives (see **O is for Objectives**), which will result in the mentee actually doing something. This can then be monitored and reflected upon at subsequent meetings.

Finally, please remember that mentoring and coaching are not always the most appropriate form of learning or leadership. When your driving instructor sees you heading into the path of an oncoming lorry, he is unlikely to ask you a good question (unless it's 'What the ★★★★ do you think you're doing?!!'). Sometimes we need to be told what to do (see **C is for Consult or Control**). But knowing when to help people learn for themselves is the mark of a good manager.

M is for Mergers

One of the inevitable consequences of applying the rules of the **Market** to FE provision has been an increase in the rate of college mergers since 1992 – the Year of Incorporation. Since mergers involve the joining of at least two previously separate institutions, and therefore inevitably some degree of restructuring of staff, the process of merger is never a comfortable one, however compelling the arguments in favour. The effect on staff is often a sinking of morale and a rise in **stress** levels. This is inevitable when an organization faces **change**; but some sources of worry are specific to the rumour or reality of merger, and can apply to personnel in any of the colleges involved. Worries arise because:

- uncertainty about the future of their job or role causes stress.
- people generally don't welcome change over which they have no control.
- the threat of losing the identity of an organization to which they feel a sense of belonging can undermine people's sense of purpose and self-esteem.
- if people aren't sure of the facts they may fear the worst.
- mergers are rarely literally that. They are usually a takeover of sorts, and everyone knows it.
- sometimes mergers involve different travel arrangements to new sites: staff may be apprehensive about the long-term effects of any moves.
- they're scared they're going to lose you and get someone worse as a manager. Better the devil they know . . .

Inevitably, people become preoccupied with 'me' issues, such as 'What will happen to my grade/salary/promotion prospects/special responsibilities/work location/early retirement plans?' In order to prevent all of this stress and uncertainty having too great an impact on team performance and output, you will have to find strategies to manage it. The lower down the management chain you are, the more difficult this will be, as you yourself may not be entirely in the know about how all of this will pan out, and you may be sharing the same uncertainties as your team. (On the other hand, if it's any consolation, the higher up the management chain you are, the more likely you will have to compete directly for your post.)

If you are ever in this situation of managing during a proposed or actual merger, here are some golden rules:

- clear and frequent communication is the best way to counteract rumour.
- transparent processes are the best way to counteract distrust.
- a positive attitude is the best way to prevent morale from plummeting.
- if there are new sites or staff involved, it may be helpful to make early group arrangements for visits to find out key facts about the merger.
- being available and approachable to listen to people's fears and concerns is the best way to keep in touch with grassroots feeling (see **W is for Walking Around**).

Not surprisingly, a college's most able and talented staff will be the first to leave if this uncertainty is not managed appropriately. So this is not about being warm and cuddly, it is about maximizing the effectiveness of the newly formed institution by treating people with respect, understanding their legitimate concerns and moving quickly to integrate people, processes and structures. Indeed, by treading too lightly and delaying tough decisions in the interests of sensitivity, management may unwittingly do staff a disservice and increase the stress on the new organization.

The issues you could have to deal with in a post-merger situation will therefore test your management skills to the utmost. Again, if you are a middle manager, they are likely to be largely about stress levels and morale, as well as numerous individual concerns about practical matters like job descriptions, staff working arrangements, travel, etc. You'll have to manage the processes whereby individuals from different institutional cultures 'gel' to form effectively functioning new teams; decisions about curriculum expertise and overlap; possibly unfamiliar environments; and probably unfamiliar line managers. All of this will require you to be adept at managing your own stress levels (see **S is for Stress**).

M is for Mission Statement

Are you familiar with your college's Mission Statement? Perhaps you had a hand in drafting or re-drafting it. The Mission Statement is now a requirement. It is a statement of intent against which college achievement may be measured. In other words, the college is as answerable for its Mission Statement as Captain Kirk was for his declared intent to boldly go where no one has gone before. Though life as an FE manager may sometimes seem like something out of science fiction, it's got to feel easy in comparison with that.

N is for Negotiation

Zoë, a recently appointed team leader, ambushes her Section Head, Norman, over a coffee in the staffroom.

ZOË Norman, I've just heard Raj is being sent to the conference on self-assessment in London next month.

NORMAN Well . . . not exactly. He asked me a couple of months ago if he could attend, and I couldn't see any good reason why not, so . . .

ZOË So, how much money is left in our staff development budget then?

NORMAN Oh, there's still quite a bit. Well . . . when I say quite a bit, I mean, you know, there's some . . .

ZOË So why did you stop me going on that course on new curriculum requirements? I'm supposed to have special responsibility for that in this job.

NORMAN Look, Zoë, you weren't section leader when you asked about that, and anyway it was in Edinburgh, and there's sure to be more of these sessions nearer home, which wouldn't cost so much.

ZOË Haven't you got to spend that budget by next month, or risk a reduction next year?

NORMAN Blimey, you have done your homework, haven't you? Be that as it may, there are other people with equally legitimate claims on these funds. I've got to be fair to everyone.

ZOË So, who else's development requests are you considering?

NORMAN Ah, well . . . now . . . it wouldn't really be fair of me to say . . . Look, don't look at me like that. I've said no, and that's that.

ZOË   So, I have a genuine job need to attend this event, which
             is more than can be said for Raj. And it would improve
             my contribution to the whole curriculum debate
             hugely, but you're prepared to look as though you're
             discriminating against a female member of staff. Is it the
             hotel costs you're worried about?

NORMAN   Yes, that's exactly it. Edinburgh's incredibly expensive.

ZOË   Well, I've got family in Edinburgh. What if I stay with
             them? Then you've only got to cover the conference
             costs.

NORMAN   OK, I suppose that would be all right. Go ahead and
             book it, then.

ZOË   Great! Thanks. I'll have to fly up, because I'm teaching
             that afternoon . . .

As managers, we can often find ourselves in what might loosely be
called negotiations, whether informally, like this, or in a more formal context, over the timing of leave or the re-allocation of
responsibilities, for example. Negotiation is the process of resolving
conflict through compromise. By definition, this usually means
both sides conceding something to the other. The final balance of
concessions is what determines the success or otherwise of the
discussion.

So what are some of the elements which affect the outcome of
this encounter, and why is Norman so badly wrong-footed? Is this
an example of a successful negotiation or not?

Let's look first at what you need to do to negotiate successfully.

Identify your objectives

- Be clear about exactly what you want to achieve from the
  discussion. Zoë had decided what she wanted. (And it looks as
  though a free visit to her family may have come into this
  somehow.) But Norman had no time to think what his
  objectives were.
- Try to divide the objectives into an ideal outcome, an acceptable outcome and a minimum fallback position. Have some
  idea before you start about what you can and cannot concede.

Identify key bargaining points
- These are the commitments you need to gain in order to move towards your overall objectives. In Zoë's case, she wanted to get Norman to admit that hotel costs were a key barrier. She also had a bargaining point about fairness, to do with her and Raj's relative needs.

Identify common ground
- Thinking about the other party's objectives as well as your own should enable you to identify where there may be common ground and where you may be able to extend it.
- You can then use this as a point to return to, if discussions get bogged down, or as a launch pad for a new proposal, counter-proposal, agreement or adjournment. Zoë had spotted that spending the outstanding budget may be an area of common ground.

Ask questions
- Good negotiators ask twice as many questions, and listen hard. They want to find out information, rather than give it away. (You'll notice Norman asks only one question, and that's rhetorical.) Good general communication skills are vital to successful negotiation; not only questioning and listening, but summarizing and checking understanding as well (see **I is for Interview**).
- Use different sorts of questions to seek information, gain clarification and test for commitment.

Prepare your case
- Generally, people will shift their position in a negotiation if:
  - they feel they have no option
  - remaining where they are will be unpleasant for them
  - they can see some real benefit in moving
- So, prepare with these in mind:
  - identify the strengths, facts which support your case, compelling arguments, previous custom and practice.
  - think of the unpleasant consequences if your proposals are not agreed with (but be careful with this one! Norman sometimes doesn't get this right. See **B is for Bullying**).

- what are the benefits for everyone if they were to agree with your arguments?

(Can you see where Zoë made all three of these types of preparation?)

- In complicated or delicate cases, make notes.
  - ○ it's helpful to have an aide-memoire of the points you want to make, but stick to just a few powerful ones.
- Identify your weaknesses and/or the other party's strengths.
  - ○ try to anticipate what arguments the other person may run and how you will respond.

Present your case

- Use common ground and key bargaining points to launch your case.
- Use your arguments to paint a compelling picture of what you want, and include the other party in it.
- But don't reveal all your points up front. Keep something in reserve.
- Follow some sort of structure:
  - – *Exploring*: questioning to gain information and test commitments. Listening to the other's case fully, without necessarily reacting. Making your case and agreeing an agenda of issues.
  - – *Expectation*: use benefits and consequences of non-acceptance, but apply power gently at first, to avoid antagonizing. Summarize arguments so far. Highlight common ground. Listen for signals of possible movement. Give signals of your own about where you may make concessions.
  - – *Moving*: make realistic proposals and move only small amounts as necessary. Leave yourself room to manoeuvre. Let the other person make their proposals fully without interruption. Make any proposals conditional on concessions from the other party.
  - – *Concluding*: is this the right moment, or is it too soon for the other person? Summarize any agreement in detail, with points of clarification and agreement.

So was Zoë and Norman's discussion a successful negotiation?

That really depends on how you view the outcome. Did Zoë 'win' and Norman 'lose'? (win–lose) or did they both lose? (lose–lose) or did they both win? (win–win).

We all know of situations, public or private, where the other side has been beaten into submission, or duped. However, the sign of a successful negotiation, especially informally within the team, is that relationships are maintained for the long term, and this means trying to achieve a win–win result. So, however shrewdly Zoë may have prepared and presented her case, if you think she has left Norman feeling mugged, then the negotiation was, to a degree, unsuccessful.

O is for Objectives

There are many aspects of managing a team, from appraisal and coaching to problem-solving and project management, where the ability to agree on clear objectives makes all the difference to the success of the exercise. How can we ensure that we establish and articulate these objectives as effectively as possible?

Let's look at an example. Here's Norman again:

What I want you to do, Angela, is see that our key local employer contacts are briefed about what's going on at the college. Make 'em feel kept in the loop. You know the sort of thing. Maybe a few sandwiches. . . . Oh, and a bit of a slide show, eh? Re-use my stuff from last time.

Is this a good-quality piece of objective-setting? Clearly not, but this sort of thing is what passes for an objective among busy managers in many organizations. So how can we do better? You may have come across the following helpful acronym:

S pecific	clarify exactly what it is you want to happen.
M easurable	ensure that you have some way of determining whether you have been successful in making this happen.
A greed	setting objectives generally involves more than one person. The most motivating objectives are those that we agree to voluntarily.
R ealistic	to move us to action, objectives have to be achievable. They can be stretching, but they must be realistic.
T ime-bound	when does this have to happen by? Failing other hard measures, most tasks can at least be assessed against an agreed deadline.

(Sometimes people add ER to the end of this, signifying the

need for Evaluation and Review, and making the acronym SMARTER.)

If we were to apply the SMART approach to our example, we'd perhaps get Sarah to brief Angela. Having discussed what is involved, the conclusion might look something like this:

OK, Angela, so you're going to organize two similar events, on separate dates, when all local employers who are offering work experience for students at the college will be invited to a briefing on the reorganization. The purpose here is to send them away understanding who their new points of contact are and which course structures may alter. Both sessions need to have taken place before the end of April, and if they're successful we'll have briefed at least 75 per cent of the targeted employers and received a majority of good or excellent ratings on our event feedback sheets. Are you happy with all this?

Apart from conforming more to the requirements of the SMART model, two other characteristics distinguish this version from our first attempt. It has clearly been co-created as part of a two-way discussion between Angela and her boss, rather than issued as an instruction (even a rather vague one, like Norman's).

Secondly, although Angela is given a much clearer brief about what she must achieve, she is actually given greater freedom in how she goes about achieving it. Enabling people to act on their own initiative often means agreeing clear structures and standards that they can work to.

P is for Paperwork

Question: *What do you call someone who's standing up to their neck in paperwork?*
Answer: *A manager in FE.*

Paperwork seems a quaint term in these electronic times. But whether the forms and returns and reports and audits and evaluations and all the rest are steadily accumulating in your email inbox or in a wire tray, the effect is the same: paperwork clamours for your attention, whatever else you're doing.

To deal with it, you'll need to draw on a range of managerial skills, most of which you'll find in this A–Z. They include:

- *Getting organized*: making considered judgements about what can or can't wait; for example, whether externally generated paperwork (e.g. from LSC or Ofsted) should always be treated as more urgent than internal forms or responses.
- *Delegation*: but don't forget that your team are most likely to be already inundated with paperwork of their own. The trick here is to use individual knowledge and expertise within the team while avoiding log-jams by not always overloading the same people. There may also occasionally be the opportunity to delegate upwards.
- *Time management*: paperwork is never finished. You can never cross that final return off the 'to do' list and sit back with a contented sigh. Managers who've come to terms with this fact and have organized their time to shift as much as they can, when they can, are happier managers.

Perhaps the most important piece of accumulated wisdom, gleaned from all the FE managers we've spoken to, is: *Never try to solve a problem by just creating more paperwork. There may be another way.*

P is for Performance Management

For any line manager in FE, a perennial problem is how to meet constantly changing curriculum demands (such as working to revised assessment criteria or teaching 14–16 year-olds) while at the same time helping colleagues to develop their skills and career prospects; how to deploy staff to achieve organizational goals, while also encouraging them to develop to their full potential. A formal system of performance review is central to this key management task (see **A is for Appraisal**). But what happens when we find ourselves dealing with staff who we know are performing badly? How do we manage poor performance?

As we suggest in the section on **Appraisal**, a formal performance discussion once a year, however cleverly designed, will never have much impact. Formal appraisal works best when it is integrated into a wider framework of performance management. We tend to feel motivated when we experience a sense of purpose, achievement and recognition. So effective managers should ask themselves:

Sense of purpose
- Do I understand what I and my team are really here for?
- How do we contribute to the overall aims of the college?
- What are the key result areas that make up this contribution?
- How are they measured?
- Do I regularly communicate all this to my team and ensure they understand it?

Achievement
- What are the agreed standards to which I and my team should perform?
- What are the measurable targets we have agreed to meet?

- How am I ensuring that my team contribute to these, and remain committed to them?
- Do I set a good example for others to follow?
- How am I ensuring that individuals are stretched to fulfil their potential?

Recognition

- When did I last praise a member of my team for doing something well?
- Was I specific and did I give an example?
- Am I confronting unacceptable behaviour/performance promptly?
- Was I specific and did I give an example? Did I offer to help?

Internal quality systems such as self-assessment and external inspection (for example by Ofsted and QAA) are often means of identifying areas of excellence in most colleges. Unfortunately, these same processes can occasionally result in the identification of staff who are judged to be 'failing'. Most managers in an FE college, and certainly most of the people working within a particular section, are well aware of who the 'good' teachers are and – if there are any – who are not. There is usually a wide variety of sources which provide informal feedback on individual performance. These may include student comment, letters of complaint, attendance and retention figures, peer observation, achievement figures or exam results and so on. In discovering that one of your team is under-performing or perhaps even struggling, you, as manager, have several options. You can:

- do nothing, in the hope that the problem will go away – usually a false hope, and sometimes a coward's way out of a possibly awkward confrontation.
- seek improvement by enlisting staff development resources.
- consider transferring the member of staff to other work which might allow them to play to their strengths.
- as a final resort, use the **disciplinary** process, recognizing that a possible final outcome could be dismissal of the colleague involved.

To establish whether what you're dealing with can formally be identified as poor performance, you will need to look at the evidence. Weightman (1999) identifies a number of specific steps you might take as part of this process.

- establish what criteria should be met in order for a performance to qualify as satisfactory.
- gather reliable and current information about actual performance.
- identify whether the gap between required and actual performance is such as to merit intervention.
- determine the reason for the gap.
- plan a course of action to deal with the problem.

There is no cure-all for poor performance, for the simple reason that it can arise from such a broad range of causes, from ill-health to inadequate professional development. As a manager, you have a number of strategies at your disposal for addressing poor performance in your team, most of which are listed in this A–Z. They include **appraisal, feedback**, continuing professional development (CPD) and – as an extreme measure – the **disciplinary** procedure.

P is for Politics

Parveen, Head of Health and Social Care, is emailing Norman, Head of Travel & Tourism. She has copied in Sarah, Head of Faculty and Norman's boss.

Norman,

Thanks for your recent note requesting that I find some way of releasing Harry from his Wednesday afternoon classes to attend your Basic Skills working party. I was surprised that you had spoken to Harry about the possibility of joining this, without consulting with me first.

I'm sure you will appreciate that, as a Centre of Vocational Excellence, my School is currently under a lot of pressure from the Principal and Corporation to increase student numbers, particularly as areas like your own are suffering a bit of a retention struggle at present. I am, as we speak, trying to persuade the college to increase my School staffing budget in order to accommodate this planned expansion.

Obviously, I do not wish to deprive Harry of the opportunity to participate in a cross-faculty team, or prevent you from delivering such a high-profile project. However, without additional resource, I find it difficult to see how I might justify agreeing to your request.

Yours,

Parveen

Ouch! Is this what we mean by being 'political'? Parveen is certainly displaying many of the 'games' of a seasoned operator here: building territory and consolidating her powerbase, while undermining her competitor in the resources stakes and dropping him in it with his boss, to boot. Our lingering sense (and probably Norman's) is that she must have more than her stated agenda in mind.

So do you wholeheartedly embrace a political perspective on organizations, as communities, like any other, racked with divisions between different interest groups, all fighting for position, power and resources? Or do you see politics as a destructive by-product of any organized group, which is to be confronted and overcome by virtuous managers in the interests of everyone? Either way, there is no doubt that organizations, and certainly organizations as large and diverse as most colleges, cannot entirely avoid internal politics.

After all, colleges are made up of people, with different values and opinions, perhaps conflicting priorities and goals, and numerous informal alliances, all trying to use limited resources, hopefully to do the best job they can for the students. If we see 'politics' as, on the one hand, people finding ways to exercise power and influence, and, on the other, differences of interests, priorities or opinion leading to conflict, then 'politics' are neither avoidable nor necessarily a bad thing.

As managers, we are partly there to create some sort of order in this environment. It is the choices we make about how to do this that will determine the degree of conflict and whether it has a negative or positive impact. Politics and conflict can be an insidious distraction, preventing productive work. But conflict can also be a force for innovation, performance improvement and change. So this is something of a trade off. How can we balance common goals and consensus with questioning and diversity in order to harness conflict more effectively, turning destructive back-stabbing into fruitful debate?

First we must study our own motives. Are we looking for constructive challenge or 'Yes people'? a solution or a victory? Do we believe in striving for a 'win–win' outcome? (see **N is for Negotiation**). Is Parveen seeking a joint solution with Norman, or simply defending her patch? Are our team's best interests served by competition and a struggle for control or by collaboration in helping each other achieve a mutually acceptable outcome?

Our approach will partly be determined by the conditions created in the college. Collaboration will be encouraged by:

- having clarity around roles and responsibilities
- sparing use of rules and procedures
- a physical layout which discourages territorial instincts
- systems which facilitate sharing of information
- performance measures which are common and fair
- a trusting environment where mistakes are tolerated

- team goals which are aligned with a shared vision for the whole organization (see **A is for Accountability**)

Think about what opportunities the team gets to interact. People isolated on different sites, with little opportunity for face-to-face communication with colleagues, will easily invent hidden agendas and conspiracy theories to fill in gaps in their information. Generally, if the conditions are right, our behaviour towards colleagues is likely to be more constructive. But a college may even consider having explicit shared values and ground rules governing how individuals behave towards each other to ensure that conflict is positively channelled. This could form part of the Culture of **Respect**. Here are some thoughts to get started:

- criticize ideas, not individuals
- don't accuse people who are not there to answer
- focus on team goals
- be prepared to learn
- ask questions and listen
- help others contribute
- clarify understanding and seek solutions instead of getting defensive
- use appropriate communication (e.g. don't send an email if it's sensitive. Talk to them.)
- demonstrate mutual respect
- observe common social courtesies (e.g. greet and ask after people)
- avoid favouritism

You can read more about organizational politics in: Handy (1999), Morgan (1998), Hatch (1997); and more about constructive team-working can be found in West (2004).

P is for Colin Powell

OK, so you may take the view that the retired Chairman of the US Joint Chiefs of Staff has nothing to teach you that you want to hear. However, you don't get to be the first African-American to fill the most senior job in the US Armed Services without gaining some useful insights into leadership . . . even if you do pronounce your name funny.

If you want to read what the General has to say in full, then read the book (Harari 2002) but for now, here are a few observations which struck a chord with us:

- Good leaders are accessible. When those whom you lead stop bringing you their problems, then you've failed as a leader, because they have either lost confidence in your ability to help, or you have persuaded them that asking for help is a sign of weakness.
- If you believe in always waiting for official permission to try things out, you will always find somebody to say 'no'. Good leaders take the view that they can always try something new, provided they haven't actually been told not to. In other words, they take the initiative.
- Keep it simple. A hallmark of good leadership is the ability to live with ambiguity yourself while creating a clear, compelling vision for your followers. Leaders help people see the wood for the trees.
- If you wait until you have 100 per cent of the information required for a decision or course of action, you will never do anything. Probability of success increases in line with the information available, but once you are in the 40–70 per cent arena, then 'go with your gut'. It may be riskier to procrastinate.

- No matter how participative and involving your style, the leader must bear the responsibility for success or failure. So prepare to be lonely.

(Adapted from *The Leadership Secrets of Colin Powell* by Oren Harari (2002).)

Q is for Quality

This is a word we hear a great deal in FE. The changes in funding to FE post-Incorporation have brought with them a move towards a consumer culture in which education and training provision is required to meet standards of quality demanded by the 'customer' (see **M is for Market**) while continuing to operate within budgetary constraints. 'Quality', however, is rather a slippery term. It used to be associated with rank and luxury (remember the ladies and gents on those tins of Quality Street?); but in terms of management, quality is now measured by the level to which a product or service meets the needs of the customer. In terms of Total Quality Management (TQM) this is sometimes referred to as fitness for purpose. Applying TQM to college provision gives us three criteria for deciding whether an aspect of provision is achieving good 'Quality'. These are:

- whether it does the job that it was intended to do
- whether it's cost-effective
- whether it can be easily accessed

In other words, Quality is defined by the requirements of our 'users' and clients, rather than by the college itself. There are some difficulties, as you'll see at once, in taking these definitions which originally related to a profit-making commercial context and applying them to an education and training organization. What, for example, do we mean when we ask, *Does the provision do the job it was meant to do?* Are we talking about outcomes? Learner satisfaction? Employer satisfaction? Qualification rates? Progression rates? All of these? What job exactly is our provision meant to do? Defining quality outcomes in an FE context is not as straightforward as defining quality outcomes in a shoe factory; not least because it is often unclear whom we should regard as the end user. Is it the learner?

The learner's employer? The LSC? In some sense it's all of these and others, too.

Most of the time, however, we are saved from this philosophical debate by the use of Performance Indicators (PIs), Inspection Frameworks and the quality frameworks of awarding bodies. And in many colleges, we now have a Quality Manager whose role is to coordinate, monitor and manage quality assurance across all aspects of the college's provision. Your own responsibilities as a manager are likely to include the monitoring and assessment of quality, which may take a variety of forms, from the gathering of retention and achievement data to the observation of individuals' practical teaching.

R is for Recruitment

Contributing to decisions about recruitment and appointment is one of the most important jobs that a manager in FE has to do, even though at times this may seem like just a peripheral part of your role. Staffing is by far the largest element of college budgets, and therefore appointment of the wrong person can be an expensive mistake.

Recruitment and Selection are part of the process of integrating the human resource requirement into the college's overall plans and objectives. This requirement is encapsulated in the college long-term plan, which is then translated at faculty, department or school level to a faculty/department/school plan. This has to attempt the difficult task of forecasting the future size and shape of the curriculum, in three or five years' time, perhaps; and from this the ideal staff profile can be defined. This can be described as strategic human resource planning.

One of the first tasks for a line manager wishing to recruit new staff is to justify the appointment to senior management. For example, let's look at Sarah who, as Head of Sports and Leisure Studies, is deciding what to do about a vacant post for a lecturer in Travel and Tourism. The current post-holder is about to move on to a senior post elsewhere, having worked in the department for ten years on a wide range of programmes, from Adult Basic Skills to HNC and has acted as Work Experience Coordinator across all programmes. Sarah now has to choose which of the following options she should go for:

- Ask for a full-time replacement using the same job description?
- Re-allocate the work among existing staff and save the salary?

- Reorganize the job description and ask for additional staff in another curriculum area?
- Recruit part-time staff to cover her work?

Whichever choice Sarah makes, she'll have to justify her recommendation to senior management in terms of cost effectiveness, student recruitment and strategic planning. The process may involve a job analysis, the outcome of which is the production of a job description or specification. Then the next step is to define the type of person who will best fit this job – this is the Person Specification. This will typically contain details of essential and desirable qualifications and experience, together with personal qualities and aptitudes.

The job and person specifications will form the basis for drafting an appropriate advertisement for a job. After application letters are received, the selection process begins. This almost always includes an interview (see **I is for Interview**), perhaps in conjunction with some other method such as psychometric testing, a presentation, a 'live' teaching session, or a simulated task associated with the job. To find out more about selection interview techniques, see **S is for Selection**.

In having some input in the recruitment of your team, you will be contributing to decisions which will affect your working life as a manager perhaps for many years.

R is for Respect

There are two senses in which Respect is a key issue for any manager in FE. The first, which is about carrying out your role in such a way as to earn the respect of colleagues, and particularly those whom you manage, we deal with this in some detail under **A is for Authenticity, E is for Emotional Intelligence** and **L is for Leadership**. The other sense in which Respect becomes part of your remit as a manager is to be found in the phrase *Culture of Respect*. This is an expression increasingly in use in political discourse about education; and in many colleges it has become translated into a Policy of Respect which sets out for the benefit of learners the rules governing acceptable behaviour on the college premises. This may involve such regulations as: no mobile phone use during lessons; no smoking except in designated areas; no use of offensive language on college premises; and so on. Whether your college refers to it in such terms or not, there will certainly be a behaviour policy or set of rules of some kind which it is your responsibility as a manager to uphold and enforce. What this means in simple terms is that you may be drawn into situations in which members of your team are experiencing problems with managing the behaviour of a learner or learners; or where a group or an individual may need to receive a warning or be informed of sanctions such as the withholding of the EMA (Educational Maintenance Allowance). In such situations you may find the following guidelines useful.

- *Always model the behaviour you expect to see.* For example, avoid such commands as: 'Don't f***ing swear at me!' And if there's a *No Phones, No Smoking* policy, don't light up and phone home until you're off the premises.
- *Avoid confrontation and escalation.* If you need to reprimand a

learner, choose your moment and remember that even in this aspect of your role you should still be aiming to provide a model of reasonable and civilized (albeit firm and authoritative) behaviour.

- *Know when to turn a blind eye.* Chasing up every minor misdemeanour will not only leave you no time for anything else, but will also devalue the effectiveness of your wrath or disapproval. It's about having a sense of scale, and making sure your team shares the same realistic set of priorities; so that if any of you are really going to read the riot act, you save it for something serious like bullying, rather than a minor infringement of dress code. This doesn't mean, however, that you should decide for yourself which rules count. Rules are rules; and as a manager it's your responsibility to uphold them (see **Z is for Zero Tolerance**).
- *Be fair, and be seen to be fair.* This is one of the best ways to foster a culture of Respect.
- *Behave towards others with respect,* whatever their status. This is the most effective way to gain respect for yourself.

S is for Selection

Norman is Head of the School of Travel and Tourism. Selecting a new departmental Admin Assistant has not been top of his priority list, but a series of disastrous temps has forced him to put aside some time and do some interviews. For him, as for many of us, this is only an occasional duty, and for that reason, feels rather unfamiliar.

NORMAN   Are you here for the interview?

OLIVIER   Yes, I'm not sure if . . .

NORMAN   Great stuff. Let's just see if this room's being used. Doesn't look like it. Don't worry about the noise. The sheet-metal work class finishes at three. Have a seat.

OLIVIER   I wasn't sure if this was the right place. The lady on the phone wasn't too specific.

NORMAN   Mmm . . . Good, good . . . Sorry, I'm just reading your CV . . . You don't seem to have stayed in jobs very long. Why is that? Do you find it hard to settle, or do you just get bored easily?

OLIVIER   Well, neither really. My wife is a Retail Manager and used to get moved around from branch to branch. But now she's in a Head Office job.

NORMAN   Following your wife around, eh? That must stick in the craw a bit?

OLIVIER   It was frustrating sometimes, but she is the major breadwinner, and my job allows me to work more flexible hours and look after the kids.

NORMAN   But you don't mind all that, and being an admin assistant, even though you're a bloke? Is it a French thing? You are French, I take it?

OLIVIER   My mother is French, and no, I enjoy my work. I'm

expert at all the basic Office applications, good with
people and I'm well-organized.

NORMAN   I've just noticed here it says you were in the army.

OLIVIER   Yes, for three years, before I was married. I worked
mainly in Stores and Logistics for the Royal Engineers.

NORMAN   Good for you, son. Best training you can get. Ah,
here's Personnel, at last. I think we've found our man,
Simon . . .

You may have spotted a few unconventional aspects to Norman's
selection interviewing style. You may even have run into him yourself (or wanted to). Having looked earlier at some of the generic
skills of interviewing, use this section to remind yourself of the
specific issues around reaching selection decisions. We have divided
this into: Preparation, Structure, Questioning, Recording and
Pitfalls.

Preparation

As Norman ably demonstrates, preparation can make the difference
between an effective and highly professional job and car-crash management. First of all, before any selection takes place, a job description for the vacant role and an agreed person specification should
be drawn up (see **R is for Recruitment**). This can be used to
determine which criteria (e.g. experience, qualifications, com-
petences, personality attributes, personal circumstances etc.), the
process is intended to assess.

Of course, unlike Norman, *you* will have read CVs or application
forms from any candidates *before* any interview takes place, and
determined any questions arising from the contents. These may
include:

- clarification of gaps in employment history
- further details in support of a candidate's suitability
- probing of particular areas of concern, such as salary, mobility,
  etc.

During the selection process, it also helps to think what information candidates will want to receive:

- key aspects of the role, e.g. copy of advert

- some data on the location
- overview of selection process and timings
- map of location
- general information about the college

In preparing for interviews, there will always be specific questions you wish to ask each particular candidate, but there is some benefit in standardizing as much of the interview as possible. This makes comparisons more objective and helps to avoid the influence of the 'halo' effect (see page 122).

Structure

Provided that the selection interview is structured and reasonably consistent, the exact model used can remain a matter of personal style. Common approaches are:

Biographical
'So tell me about school and university. What made you study xyz?'

Career path
'Let's begin by talking about your current job, then you can tell me how your previous career led up to this.'

Competency
'Tell me about an occasion when you have helped a member of your team improve their performance.'

Or, for the Admin Assistant post: 'Tell me how, in your previous experience, you've handled a situation where . . .'

Questioning

Use largely open questions to gather information, with occasional closed questioning to check facts or probe a particular issue.

When assessing competencies, try using 'critical incident' questions, as this challenges the candidate to talk about real life events rather than just give opinions. Wherever possible, candidates should be pressed to give examples of situations/activities from their own experience which provide evidence of what they are saying about themselves.

You may wish to challenge candidates and probe ambiguities

or evasions. But avoid high-pressure questioning techniques and bullying of candidates, as this rarely helps you gain the maximum information from the interviewee and damages your reputation as an employer.

Recording

You should try to record as much detail as possible of the evidence provided by the candidate during the interview, to ensure accurate assessment and allow detailed feedback to the candidate. Do this either during the interview (with the candidate's permission) or immediately afterwards.

Pitfalls

Legal requirements

- you must avoid discrimination on the grounds of race, colour, nationality, gender, marital status, age, sexual orientation or disability.
- questioning must be directly relevant to the job and equally relevant to all candidates.

Personal motivation and emotion

- one is quick to perceive one's own faults in others.
- our expectations, realistic or otherwise, may affect our judgement.

Abstract characteristics

- you can judge verbal fluency, self-confidence, sense of humour.
- but how will you judge honesty, integrity, sincerity?

Non-verbal cues

- does the body language confirm or contradict what is being said?

Halo effect

- when our judgement on a range of dimensions is swayed by a single dominant positive attribute. So instead of evaluating the person 'warts and all', the person is judged to be an all-round 'good egg'. (Once Norman knows about Olivier's army background, he can do no wrong.)

Rush to judgement

- avoid making your decision on first impressions only. First impressions stick – often regardless of later evidence. Judgements and decisions about people's characteristics are made within a matter of minutes and contradictory information is frequently ignored.

Lack of concentration

- it is very difficult to observe or listen continuously and human attention is notoriously selective. When concentration lapses we tend to reconstruct what we think we heard, or wanted to hear.

Stereotypes

- stereotypes operate when a single characteristic of an object or person brings to mind a cluster of other qualities supposedly linked to that characteristic, e.g. 'if a person has red hair, they have a hot temper'.

Prejudice

- where you judge a person solely on the basis of a single characteristic, such as race or gender, or age. Few people can honestly claim to be free of all prejudices, so it is important that you remain self-aware (see **E is for Equal Opportunities**).

Attribution

- we all have a tendency to explain our own poor performance in terms of situations and circumstances, but other people's in terms of motives and personality traits ('I lost it a bit with Angela the other evening. I'd just had a really hard week. You should have heard what she said to me, though. She hasn't half got a temper on her!')

S is for Shackleton

What is a polar explorer doing in an *A–Z* for FE managers? In fact, Ernest Shackleton's name crops up a lot these days in the context of leadership and people management (for example Morrell and Capparell 2001 and Alexander 1999). He's become something of a leadership and management icon because, in getting his entire crew back safely from a disastrous Antarctic expedition, he demonstrated a set of skills and qualities which would be useful to anyone who leads a team of people in any context. His famous declaration: 'Not a life lost, and we have been through hell', might sum up many a manager's sentiments following a full-scale Ofsted inspection. In FE parlance, Shackleton (1874–1922) possessed what we might term transferable skills. They include:

- motivating the team under difficult circumstances by using praise, trust and an emphasis on team spirit
- focusing on the collective and individual goals of the team, rather than his own personal goals or those of financial backers
- maintaining self-control, even under provocation
- building up the self-esteem of team members
- practising what he preaches and modelling effective practice
- combining firm, directive leadership with emotional intelligence

These aspects of Shackleton's management style have been contrasted with those of the notorious Captain Bligh, set adrift by the mutineers of the *Bounty* (Wallace 2002). He, too, brought the remnants of his crew in an open boat through a perilous voyage to eventual safety. But whereas Shackleton was honoured – almost worshipped – by his team for his leadership qualities, Bligh seems only to have earned the unanimous loathing of the men whose lives he saved. This may be due in part to the fact that his style seems to have been the diametric opposite in almost every way to Shackleton's. For example, according to the members of his crew whom he saved, the notable aspects of his style consisted in:

- motivating the crew under difficult circumstances by using threats, encouraging dependency and warning them that they'd be lost without him as only he had the skills to navigate them to safety
- focusing on his own personal goal of bringing the mutineers to justice
- losing self-control under provocation
- undermining the self-esteem of crew members
- taking an elitist position and failing to provide an appropriate model of behaviour
- combining directive leadership with a lack of consideration of the impact of his behaviour and decisions on the state of mind of his crew

We suggested that Shackleton and Bligh were opposites in *almost* every way. One way in which they were very similar was in their directive, top-down, almost autocratic style of management. The fact that Shackleton could empathize with his team and create a culture of 'us' rather than 'me and you lot' – and the fact that he was a transformational leader – doesn't mean he was a soft touch (see **T is for Transformational Leadership**). He even drew a gun on a potential mutineer and threatened to shoot him – for the sake of the rest of the team, of course. Now, we categorically do *not* advise that particular strategy. But the point we're making is that it's possible to be a directive, decisive manager who makes tough decisions and at the same time retain the trust and support of those you manage. It's no accident that we refer to Shackleton's people as a *team* and Bligh's as a *crew*.

In the interests of fairness we must point out that Bligh, too, has been held up as an exemplary leader, for example by Caroline Alexander (1999), whose presentations on Bligh and his style have apparently included one made to the Pentagon. Yes. Really.

One more important thing about Shackleton that everyone seems to forget: he never did reach his Antarctic destination. He is regarded as a hero now because his overriding achievement was to bring back every one of his team to safety. This reminds us that management is as much about adapting successfully to changing circumstances as it is about achieving preset goals; and that occasional failure to reach those goals doesn't necessarily make you a bad manager.

S is for Silver Book

Oh yes. We're open to learners twenty-four seven. We're not on The Silver Book now, you know.

Perhaps you've heard this quaint expression and wondered in passing where it comes from. Well, if you're sitting comfortably, I'll begin. Before Incorporation in 1992, lecturers' conditions of service were enshrined in a document with a silver cover, commonly referred to as The Silver Book. With Incorporation came an era when individual colleges negotiated salaries and conditions with their staff. Some lecturers who declined to sign the new contracts chose instead to forgo incremental rises in salary and to retain their old terms of employment, which included shorter hours and more holiday entitlement. They became known as Silver Book Lecturers. They are almost extinct now; but it is not beyond the bounds of possibility that you may encounter one still. It is rumoured that they might look poorer but not quite so exhausted as other members of your team.

S is for Stress

Always tired? Losing your temper with colleagues? Getting more headaches than usual? Losing sleep and experiencing feelings of powerlessness? Punched anyone recently who went on about teachers' holidays?

You may be suffering from undue stress. Of course, you'll have to join the queue . . .

What is stress?

The Health and Safety Executive defines stress as:

the adverse reaction people have to excessive pressure or other types of demand placed on them (accessed on: 17/05/06 www.hse.gov.uk/ stress).

In our work and personal lives we are constantly trying to balance the demands made upon us with the internal and external resources we have to cope with them. To a degree, stress is always with us, and this is not necessarily a bad thing. Getting a bit keyed up before an important meeting or presentation may help sharpen our performance. A certain amount of pressure contributes to us getting things done on time. Some people even claim to work at their best under pressure (especially when the boss is within earshot).

However, it is the word 'excessive' which is crucial here. When the balance tips too far towards the demands placed upon us and we cannot summon the necessary resources, then we feel 'stressed' . . . and in a bad way.

What causes stress?

Most of us know that things like moving house, divorce and retirement, not to mention family Christmases, can be major sources of stress in our everyday lives, particularly if they all come at once! To this list we can probably add bereavement, travel, financial worries, crime and many others. But what about our working lives?

What many of the above experiences have in common, is that they are often accompanied by a sense of powerlessness, an inability to determine our own fate. This is also at the root of much work-place stress. Any of these stressors sound familiar to you?

- lack of clear objectives and values or conflicting objectives
- poor communication and lack of information
- lack of consultation or involvement in change
- lack of support from one's manager
- sustained work overload
- sustained work underload
- boring and repetitive work
- inadequate skills/training. Over-promotion
- constant dealing with complaints which one is powerless to solve
- career uncertainty
- confusing responsibilities and lines of authority
- lack of recognition
- interpersonal conflict

What are the signs of stress?
Some signs we may only be able to recognize in ourselves. Others we can recognize in those who work for us or with us. They include:

Physical signs
like headaches, breathlessness, skin irritation, nausea or increased susceptibility to illness

Psychological signs
like memory lapses, inability to concentrate, difficulty making decisions, bad dreams and more frequent mistakes

Emotional signs
like irritability, moodiness, suspicion, lack of enthusiasm, loss of confidence and self-esteem, and inappropriate humour

Behavioural changes
like loss of appetite or overeating, drinking more, smoking more, taking more work home, increased absenteeism, becoming more accident-prone, lying to cover mistakes and withdrawing from relationships

We could all be forgiven for reading this list and concluding that not only are we highly stressed, but so are all of our work colleagues and everyone else we know. (Oh dear, was that inappropriate humour?) But everyone is different and certain personality factors may predispose a person to respond more negatively to certain stressors. The key here is to watch out for combinations of factors and for *changes*. The fact that I suffer from increasing memory lapses has been with me for some time and is probably a result of creeping senility rather than stress.

What should I do as a manager?
Employers, and, by extension, their managers, have a duty of care under the Health and Safety at Work Act (1974). They must take reasonable care that health is not placed at risk due to excessive and sustained levels of stress at work. Likewise, the Management of Health and Safety at Work Regulations (1999) requires managers formally to assess activities. They must ensure that the demands of the job do not exceed employees' ability to carry out the work without risk to themselves or others. If we do not, then we will lose good people and pay the price in court, as well as at work. The HSE provides guidance and management standards you can use when assessing stress in the workplace (accessed on 22/2/2006 www.hse.gov.uk/stress/).
Here are some practical things you can do:

- ensure the college has a stress policy and you know what it says, particularly about how staff voice concerns, and what counselling is available.
- regularly discuss performance with team members, remembering to praise them for a job well done.
- look at job design and workload to ensure people are given authority with accountability, and SMART objectives (see **O is for Objectives and D is for Delegation**).

- take time to discuss personal development and training needs with individuals.
- keep lines of communication open, and never ignore signs of stress. Make it something people can talk about, not a source of shame.
- read your college bullying/harassment policy and ensure you avoid behaving in this way with your staff (see **B is for Bullying**).
- if you notice a combination of behaviour changes, talk to the person and find out what is wrong.
- be supportive to those under pressure or returning after absence due to stress.
- set a good example in how you manage your own stress levels.

What can you do about your own stress?

Clearly, because everyone is different, it is difficult to be prescriptive about what may be effective for a particular individual. But here are some ideas which seem to be broadly supported:

- try to get a good night's sleep and stick to regular sleep patterns.
- exercise regularly. Physical exertion can help relieve psychological stress. Try relaxation exercises.
- watch what you eat. A healthy diet and eating regularly may help prevent stress, as will watching your caffeine and sugar intake.
- learn to manage yourself well. Separate the important from the urgent, and schedule in reflection and planning time as well as tasks (see **Getting Organized**).
- take control. Ask yourself what *you* can change, and focus on that. Stop fretting about things outside your control.
- think positive. See change as a learning opportunity.
- take a break. Have a walk round. Freeing your mind can work wonders if you are stuck on a task.
- get spiritual. Make time to listen to music, meditate, worship or whatever helps you wind down.
- ask for help. Do not suffer in silence. Talk about it.

S is for Succession Crisis

No, this is not about the House of Windsor, though there's something novel about seeing them mentioned in a book about FE management, isn't there? This crisis is concerned with the future of FE leadership, given the number of principals currently in post who are rapidly approaching retirement, and the dearth of potential replacements with appropriate backgrounds and experience of management. This crisis was one of the driving forces behind the setting up of the Centre for Excellence in Leadership (CEL) which offers professional development programmes for aspiring senior managers in FE; and to the introduction of postgraduate programmes in a number of universities which carry accreditation with an FE focus, such as Postgraduate Diplomas and MAs in Education Management. So if you're aiming for the top job and want to get yourself in line for succession (and we're still talking Principal here, not monarch), it's time to start thinking about your portfolio of qualifications and experience.

T is for Transformational Leadership

This section might equally be entitled T is for Transactional Leadership, since Transactional and Transformational leadership are two parts of the same model (Bass 1998, Avolio 1999). In its 2005 report, *Leadership, development and diversity in the learning and skills sector*, the Learning and Skills Research Centre concluded that successful organizations differed in their approach to leadership. Although a transformational leadership style was considered most effective in improving performance and in leading for diversity, managers in the sector were seen as more often employing a transactional approach. What does this mean, and why should you care?

In simple terms, transactional leadership is an exchange, as the name suggests. As manager, you understand what your team members want, and you agree roles and responsibilities, behaviours and performance standards, in return for which they are rewarded, through praise, pay, promotion, etc. You can achieve this by simply monitoring performance, and telling people off when they get it wrong ('management by exception'). However, it is generally acknowledged to work better if the manager puts more focus on recognizing and rewarding people when they do achieve what is expected of them ('contingent reward').

So, 'What's wrong with transactional leadership?' you may be asking yourself. The answer is nothing. This model is not about either–or. Having clear roles and responsibilities, SMART objectives and standards of performance, and taking the trouble to praise positive behaviour and address under-performance is all good stuff. It generally beats having no structure or standards and just letting everyone do what they like ('laissez-faire leadership'). However, the proposition is that management effectiveness is hugely increased when transactional leadership is supplemented by transformational leadership.

Transformational leaders command the trust, respect and admiration to be positive role models for their teams. They have a sense of purpose, which they share with their team, and they display determination and conviction in pursuing this. Part of this 'idealized influence' may be what people refer to as charisma, but it may also be the result of more tangible behaviours.

Transformational leaders are optimistic and positive. They paint an attractive picture of the future, and make people's work meaningful and challenging. They have high expectations.

Transformational leaders help people look at old problems in new ways, by asking challenging questions and making us think more creatively.

Finally, transformational leaders remember to focus on individual learning and development needs as well, by mentoring and coaching, delegating and just walking around talking to people (see **M is for Mentoring and Coaching, D is for Delegation, W is for Walking Around**).

Usually, when we are asked to think of great leaders (and actually when we are asked to think of great teachers), we think of these transformational qualities (see **S is for Shackleton**). It is argued that leaders who display these behaviours enable followers to achieve beyond their expectations, whereas a transactional approach will, at best, only achieve the expected outcome. Provided a degree of structure and support is in place, transformational leaders are more likely to allow people the freedom to think for themselves (laissez-faire leaders will just leave them to flounder, then blame them when they get it wrong).

Transformational leadership is not an alternative to transactional leadership. Rather it is a way of adding to its effectiveness.

U is for Updating

SARAH	Morning, Norman.
NORMAN	Morning, Sarah.
SARAH	What do you reckon to this latest White Paper on FE, then? I suppose we should have seen all that coming.
NORMAN	Er. . . . yes.
SARAH	It's going to mean more work.
NORMAN	Er. . . . more work. Yes. Absolutely. I expect so.
SARAH	Although I thought on second reading that the third section seemed to hold out the promise of more funding.
NORMAN	Oh yes. More funding. Yeah.
SARAH	We'll have to have a meeting to discuss our response to paragraphs 24 and 53, I suppose. What are your first thoughts – off the top of your head?
NORMAN	It's. . . . well, it's, it's absolutely what you said, isn't it.

This scenario may be more familiar than you would like it to be. As a matter of interest, as you read it through, which of these two managers – Head of School Norman, or Sarah, his Head of Faculty – do you find yourself empathizing with? Probably neither of them. We've all met Sarah, although probably by another name. She has an uncanny ability to make you feel inadequate and borderline illiterate because she has always read every new DfES, LSC and LLUK document the moment it's out, knows it by heart and can probably quote you page numbers. Where does she find the time? Does she never sleep? And we've probably all felt as Norman does here, at some time or another. You know there's something you're supposed to know, but if you ask about it, people will know you don't know.

So what's the answer to keeping updated without scaring your colleagues or giving up sleep? Some easy answers to this are:

- Make sure you're on all the relevant email 'updates' lists (see the list at the end of this *A–Z*). You can do this by going to the appropriate websites and registering.
- These emails (and the websites) will alert you to the publication of key documents, of which you will almost always find a summary version available on the website. The summary version may be all you need; but if not, it will guide you to the relevant sections or paragraphs you need to read in the full version.
- If you don't have time to read the education press in detail, remember that some newspapers have Education supplements or pages on certain days of the week, and all of these now include FE, so that you can get the 'edited highlights'.
- Ask your college librarian to let you know routinely when hard copies of key documents such as government White Papers become available in the library.
- Attend initiative launches and national and regional conferences when you get the chance. The college will normally pay your fee and travel expenses for these. This is where you may get the opportunity to network and to hear policy in the making, and to help shape it, too.
- Remember, you don't have to know everything, but you do need to be familiar with key points. You can ask colleagues who've read key documents already to let you have a bullet point list. It's generally better to say you don't know than to fake it like Norman. By pretending he knows all about the **White Paper**, he's trapped himself into a position now where he can't ask what he desperately needs to know.

Remaining updated is one of your professional responsibilities as a manager in FE. It's a part of your continuing professional development (CPD) in which you yourself should always be proactive. And, of course, it's also part of your responsibility to do your best to ensure that those whom you manage keep updated, too. So don't be tempted to keep such information to yourself, nor to use it for purposes of intimidation as we suspect Sarah is doing. Knowledge may well be power, but power should not be misused (see **P is for Politics**).

V is for Vice Principal

As a manager in FE, it may be that you aspire to be a VP. It may even be that you are one already, in which case brace yourself, for you are about to read some home truths about your role.

The first and foremost of these is that the VP is very often defined in relation to the Principal's management style. Whatever the job specification, if the Principal's approach is warm and hands-on and he or she knows everyone on the staff by their first name, then the odds are that the VP will be squeezed into the role of hatchet-person, the hard cop, the scary one. Conversely, a principal who prefers to keep their distance, who's happier with numbers than with names, will need a VP who can exhibit the caring side of senior management, the likeable, human approach, the good cop. These are both extremes, but you get the idea. When the Principal–VP team is working well, the strengths and the styles of the two will complement each other, as in any good partnership. If it isn't working well, then this is where we may encounter the interesting phenomenon of the 'Parked VP'. The Parked VP is so called not because he or she has been put in charge of car parks (although, sadly, this has been known to be the case), but because they appear to have no vital role in the organization structure: no line-management responsibilities; no meaningful role or responsibility in relation to curriculum, funding or personnel. They have, in other words, been 'parked'. This can be an enormous and frustrating waste of management potential and talent, engineered by an over-mighty Principal, a misguided Board, or an inappropriate organizational structure. Or it could be a strategy utilized to accommodate a VP who has not lived up to their original promise. Whatever the case, it will be clear from this that a great deal can be learned about the way a college is managed from looking at the role of its VP.

Okay, VPs. Open your eyes. You can start reading again now.

W is for Walking Around

The simple idea of 'management by walking around' has been written about by numerous authors on leadership and management, not least the renowned Peter Drucker (see **D is for Drucker**), but it is certain that the practice has been around a lot longer than this.

It may seem a statement of the obvious to suggest that managing people well involves getting off your behind and talking to them where they work, rather than always expecting them to come to you. But it is surprising how we can be seduced into spending most of our time on the things we purport to hate – answering emails, doing paperwork, sitting in meetings – rather than getting out there and talking to our team. Having an 'open-door policy' just doesn't cut it. Why should your team walk through this 'open door' if you cannot find the time to walk through in the opposite direction?

Of course, we are not all sociable extroverts by nature, who find this walking around chatting to people easy. It may feel quite a challenge, even uncomfortable. But experience suggests that this is a management behaviour which is appreciated even when done badly, provided your motives are positive. People like to see their boss making the effort, even if it does not come naturally.

Let's look at some of the things walking around allows you, as a manager, to do:

- be a visible role model
- show people you are interested in what they are doing and thinking
- take the opportunity to listen, praise and encourage
- observe the social courtesies. Ask after family. Talk about holidays
- be accessible and approachable
- answer people's questions. Reassure if possible

- reinforce the team's purpose and objectives
- identify conflict early and address appropriately
- keep learning yourself

But beware; this is a behaviour that has to be practised consistently, in order to be effective. It is an especially helpful form of communication in times of great change, it is true. But if you only walk around and talk to people in times of great change, your team will, in the manner of Pavlov's dogs, associate your visibility with bad news. Likewise, if your motivation for walking around is to spy on people and catch them up to no good, you will lose the trust and respect of your team, rather than encourage it. Think Henry V, rather than J. Edgar Hoover:

O! now, who will behold
The royal captain of this ruined band
Walking from watch to watch, from tent to tent,
Let him cry 'Praise and glory on his head!'
For forth he goes and visits all his host,
Bids them good morrow, with a modest smile,
And calls them brothers, friends and countrymen.
          (from the prologue to Act IV, Henry V, by William Shakespeare)

W is for White Papers and other milestones

Over the past couple of decades the changes to the organization, curriculum, funding and inspection of FE colleges have brought about a radical and rapid transformation of the sector. We can track these changes by looking back over the White and Green Papers, the reports and the initiatives that have triggered or signalled each new development. In this *A–Z* we have picked the **Foster Report** out for special mention, but some other major milestones have been:

- *Working Together: Education and Training* (1986): this White Paper introduced NVQs (National Vocational Qualifications) in order to rationalize the existing complex range of qualifications into a coherent framework with comparable national benchmarks.
- *Education and Training for the 21st Century* (1991): this White paper signalled the removal of colleges from local authority control; the beginnings of Incorporation; the introduction of GNVQs (General Vocational Qualifications); and the potential for schools to compete with colleges in the provision of vocational education.
- *The Dearing Review of Post-16 Qualifications* (1996): the recommendations were to preserve A levels and the general/ vocation divide, and to introduce Key Skills across the post–16 curriculum.
- *The Tomlinson Report* (1996): a milestone in the implementation of Inclusive Learning.
- *The Learning Age* (1998): set the target that all FE lecturers should undertake a professional teaching qualification. This initiative was to be supported by the FE Standards Fund.
- *Learning to Succeed* (1999): signalled the setting up of the

national and regional LSCs (Learning and Skills Councils) and their crucial role in the funding of FE (including administering the Standards Fund).

- *Success for All* (2002): a reform strategy to develop the responsiveness of the FE sector and other lifelong learning providers, with an emphasis on working with employers, 'busting bureaucracy', encouraging equality and diversity, and developing e-learning.
- *Every Child Matters* (2003): this Green Paper has had an impact on all sectors of education, with its focus on: supporting parents and carers; workforce reform; encouraging accountability and integration between services and institutions; and early intervention for the protection of young people at risk.
- *14–19 Education and Skills* (2005): the proposals of this White Paper are still rolling out in colleges. They include: the re-motivation of disengaged 14 year olds by allowing them to learn in FE colleges; a mastery of functional English and maths by all young people before they leave education; and the introduction of diplomas in 14 broad vocational areas, designed by employers through Sector Skills Councils.
- *Further Education: Raising Skills, Improving Life Chances* (2006): containing the government response to the Foster Report, this White Paper also includes new entitlements for 19–25 year-olds studying for their first Level 3 qualification, and the proposal that all new college principals should gain a leadership qualification.

You will find a list of sources at the end of this A to Z which will help you to continue your professional **updating** about future initiatives, White Papers and other publications.

X is for X-Men

X-women? X-men? OK, so now we're really getting desperate. Still, anything has got to be better than appalling puns about X-cellence or X-pertise; and basing a taxonomy of management styles around fictional superheroes is not that crazy an idea. We would like to bet that you recognize some of these managers, even if you would be well-advised not to emulate them.

Storm	flies all over the place, generating wind and fog
Professor X	communicates by telepathy. Will expect you therefore to know what he's thinking
Rogue	drains the life-force out of anyone she comes into contact with
Iceman	can reduce temperatures to sub-zero, just by walking into a room
Wolverine	poor emotional control, and when enraged (which is often), the claws really come out. Also, rather depressingly, he is virtually indestructible

Y is for You

You'll be a more effective manager if you make space to look after your own professional and personal needs.

- Take time occasionally to think about what *you* want, where you're heading, and how this fits with your hopes and aspirations. Are you where you want to be? If not, what's the first step to getting there?
- Leave room for real life. There's more to life than work, although sometimes in FE it's easy to forget this. It's important to ring-fence time – an evening or at weekends – when you not only don't talk about work but don't even *think* about it. Don't get yourself stuck into a regime of working where you have to remind your family and friends what your name is.

Z is for Zero Tolerance

Save your Zero Tolerance for the big things. As a manager in FE you should demonstrate a Zero Tolerance of:

- bullying
- discrimination
- harassment
- unprofessional behaviour
- illegal practices
- corruption
- dishonesty
- exploitation

A policy of zero tolerance will be pointless, of course, if you're seen to tolerate any of these behaviours in yourself!

And finally . . . P is for Postscript

A final word. This book has hopefully succeeded in giving you a very brief introduction to a lot of the things that will give you fun-filled days, and maybe some sleepless nights, as a manager in FE. It would be easy to get overwhelmed by the sheer volume of activities, techniques, initiatives and procedures. So, here's a very simple, last piece of advice. A cursory glance down the contents list of this *A–Z* reveals that well over 50 per cent of the topics we cover are, in essence, about your relationships with people, and how to make these more productive. The desire and ability really to connect with people is probably the aspect of leadership that would most unite all of our various heroes and gurus. Ultimately, your success as a manager will depend largely on getting the best out of others, whether they are your team, your colleagues, or your boss.

Like all managers, you will sometimes come home, kick the cat/dog/partner, feeling frustrated and fed-up, certain you have made enemies of everyone, and wasted your considerable talents on fruitless bureaucracy and 'politicking'. But, with any luck, you will have far more good days than bad. And on those days you will come home, feeling elated and fulfilled, certain that you have really contributed to the vision of the college, and made a real, positive difference in people's lives.

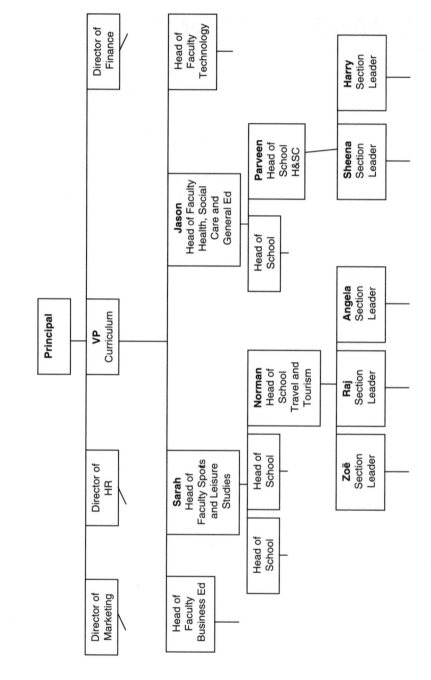

Figure 2 Part of Bassingbrook College's organization chart showing in **bold** the elements in the support chain: A to Z

References

Adair, J. (1983) *Effective Leadership*, London: Gower.

Alexander, C. (1999) *'Endurance': Shackleton's Legendary Journey to Antarctica*, London: Bloomsbury.

Avolio, B. J. (1999) *Full Leadership Development: Building the Vital Forces in Organizations*, Thousand Oaks, CA: Sage.

Barrett, R. (1998) *Liberating the Corporate Soul*, Woburn, MA: Butterworth-Heinemann.

Bass, B. M. (1998) *Transformational Leadership. Industrial, Military and Educational Impact*, Mahwah, NJ: Erlbaum.

Bennis, W. G. (1989) *On Becoming a Leader*, London, Random House.

Bennis, W. G. and Thomas, R. J. (2002) *Geeks & Geezers*, Boston, MA: Harvard Business School Press.

Blanchard, K., Zigarmi, P. and Zigarmi, D. (1986) *Leadership and the One-Minute Manager*, London: Collins.

Bridges, W. (1991) *Managing Transitions*, Reading, MA: Perseus.

Covey. S. R. (1989) *The Seven Habits of Highly Effective People*, London: Simon & Schuster.

DES (1991) *Education and Training for the 21st Century*, London: HMSO.

Drucker, P. F. (2001) *The Essential Drucker*, Woburn, MA: Butterworth-Heinemann.

Firth, D. (1999) *Smart Things to Know about Change*, Oxford: Capstone.

Gladwell, M. (2000) *The Tipping Point*, London: Little, Brown.

Goleman, D. (1996) *Emotional Intelligence*, London: Bloomsbury.

Goleman, D. (1998) *Working with Emotional Intelligence*, London: Bloomsbury.

Handy, C. (1995) *Gods of Management: The Changing Work of Organisations*, London: Arrow.

Handy, C. (1999) *Understanding Organisations*, London: Penguin.

Harari, O. (2002) *The Leadership Secrets of Colin Powell*, Maidenhead: McGraw-Hill.

Hatch, M. J. (1997) *Organization Theory*, Oxford: Oxford University Press.

Kanter, R. (1983) *Changemasters*, London: Routledge.

Kolb, D. (1983) *Experiential Learning*, Hemel Hempstead: Prentice Hall.

Kotter, J. P. (1996) *Leading Change*, Boston, MA: Harvard Business School Press.

Landsberg, M. (1996) *The Tao of Coaching*, London: HarperCollins.

Leigh, A. (1984) *20 Ways to Manage Better*, London: CIPD.

Lumby, J., Harris, A., Morrison, M., Mujis, D., Sood, K., Glover, D., Wilson, M., Briggs, A. R. J. and Middlewood, D. (2005) *Leadership, Development and Diversity in the Learning and Skills Sector*, London: Learning and Skills Research Centre.

Mehrabian, A. (1972) *Silent Messages: Implicit Communication of Emotions and Attitudes*, Belmont, CA: Wadsworth.

Morgan, G. (1998) *Images of Organization*, Thousand Oaks, CA: Sage.

Morrell, M. and Capparell, S. (2001) *Shackleton's Way*, London: Nicholas Brealey.

Owen, J. (2002) *Benchmarking for the learning and skills sector*, London: LSDA.

Schein, E. (1969) *Process Consultation: Its Role in Organisation Development*, Reading, MA: Addison Wesley.

Schein, E. (1992) *Organisational Culture and Leadership*, San Francisco, CA: Jossey-Bass.

Senge, P. (1990) *The Fifth Discipline*, London: Random House.

Torrington, D. *et al.* (2001) *Human Resource Management*, London: Prentice Hall.

Wallace, S. (2002) *Managing Behaviour and Motivating Students in FE*, Exeter: Learning Matters.

Wallace, S. and Gravells, J. (2005) *Mentoring in Further Education*, Exeter: Learning Matters.

Weightman, J. (1999) *Managing People*, London: CIPD.

West, M. (2004) *Effective Teamwork*, Oxford: BPS Blackwell.

Whitmore, J. (1992) *Coaching for Performance*, London: Nicholas Brealey.

Websites

ACAS website (Harassment/**Bullying**)
www.acas.org.uk/index.aspx?articleid=797
(accessed on 14/3/2006)
ACAS website (**Disciplinary** process)
www.acas.org.uk/index.aspx?articleid=906
(accessed on 25/4/2006)
Health and Safety Executive website (**Stress**)
www.hse.gov.uk/stress/
(accessed on 22/2/2006)

Learning Aims Database
http://providers.lsc.gov.uk/LAD
LSC Funding Guide
www.lsc.gov.uk/National/Documents/SubjectListing/Funding
Learning/FurtherEducation
LSDA website
lsda.org.uk

Sources for updating

In the section on **Updating** we suggested that you consult key websites to keep yourself up to date with current developments. The following bodies and organizations all have useful websites which you can access through the search engine of your choice. Some even have 'mailing lists' which allow you to sign up for regular email updates:

- The Association of Colleges (AoC)
- The DfES (Department for Education and Skills)
- The *Guardian* Education pages
- The Institute for Learning (IfL)
- The Learning and Skills Network (LSN)
- Lifelong Learning UK (LLUK)
- The LSC (Learning and Skills Council)
- Your local LSC
- The University and College Union (UCU), www.ucu.org.uk.
- The National Institute of Adult Continuing Education (NIACE)
- The Quality Improvement Agency (QIA)
- Standards Verification UK (SVUK)
- *The Times Educational Supplement* (*TES*)
- The Training and Development Agency (TDA)